The Suitors of Spring

The
Suitors of Spring

by
Pat Jordan

DODD, MEAD & COMPANY, NEW YORK

ISBN: 0-396-06711-5
Library of Congress Catalog Card Number: 72-9933

Printed in the United States of America
by The Cornwall Press, Inc., Cornwall, N. Y.

For Ray Cave and Patricia Ryan

Foreword

The following pieces are all profiles of baseball players, and coincidentally all the players are pitchers. Some, like Tom Seaver and Sam McDowell, are successful and famous in the major leagues today. Others, like Johnny Sain and Bo Belinsky, were once famous as pitchers but are now familiar for other reasons. Both Art DeFilippis and Steve Dalkowski are relatively unknown, although this anonymity makes them no less interesting.

Fame or obscurity had little bearing on the selections for this book. Rather, each man has a certain compelling distinctness of character. And each is, or was, a pitcher—an unintentional unifying thread I completely overlooked until it was brought to my attention by my editor, Peter Weed. He pointed out that practically all the profiles I had selected for inclusion in this "baseball book" were of pitchers. Perhaps this was only natural, for I had been a pitcher myself: a successful one as an amateur, then a failure as a professional, and finally an inactive hurler who turned to writing.

After graduating from high school in 1959, I signed a $40,000 bonus contract with the Milwaukee Braves, who promptly dispatched me to what Bo Belinsky calls "some witches' monastery in Pancakesville, Georgia." After four years in the monasteries of McCook, Waycross, Eau Claire, and Palatka, my career was as virginal and unviolated by success as the day it was born. And so, despairing, the Braves released me from my vows.

I spent the next ten years rationalizing and exorcising my failure by writing a book about my four-year pilgrimage through minor league baseball. The result, tentatively titled "The Days of Wine and Bonuses," will be published in the summer of 1974. Its writing has not only been excellent therapy but has also led me to my present career, and even more directly, to this collection of profiles. As my editor said, it was only natural that when I began writing about athletes other than myself, I should turn to pitchers. I am still fascinated by the act of pitching, which Tom Seaver believes is an art; and by its practitioners, whom Sam McDowell believes are unique among athletes.

This book, however, is not primarily concerned with pitchers and pitching, although both figure prominently. Rather, it is devoted to a close scrutiny of men who were drawn to pitching and who are interesting because of a certain distinctness transcending their talent. Hopefully, each profile tells not only about each man but also about pitching, about baseball, and most importantly about Sport itself. Each of these pitchers is seeking his proper place in Sport, and its proper place in his life. Since Sport is a universal male experience, all men, whether they wish to or not, must likewise make their peace with it. For some, as for Tom Seaver, Sport becomes "the one thing in life that excites me." For others, as for Bo Belinsky, Sport is "just a game for little boys."

PAT JORDAN

Contents

The Suitors of Spring

The bird dogs came first. They just appeared one spring day in your sophomore year of high school as if drawn by the odor of freshly cut outfield grass. On that day you knew for sure that your fastball, which had slowed considerably in the jump from a Little League to a high school mound, had once again begun to smoke like a burning pine. You knew also that your life would never be the same again. Baseball was no longer a game for you from that day forward. It was, instead, your career.

They were called bird dogs because they sniffed out talent, although the name does not do justice to the men. The bird dogs were kindly old men in plaid shirts and string ties. They owned taverns and hardware stores, and once had even played ball with Kiki Cuyler and Georgie Cutshaw. Now in their last years, they measured out the weekday afternoons at an endless succession of high school baseball games. They were always easy to spot, even from

1

the mound, since few adults bothered to watch the meaningless games your coach let you pitch as a sophomore, and because they always stood directly behind the home-plate screen, as if they would not feel comfortable unless viewing the world through a maze of wire triangles.

Few of the bird dogs ever got paid a cent for their efforts, although once in a while one would be promised a $100 bonus if the boy he touted ever made the major leagues. But even if that boy did make it, by the time he did the bird dog usually would have died. That wasn't why they went through the effort. They did it to pass time for one thing and because they loved the game for another—but most of all because they appreciated young talent. Just watching it develop was reward enough for old men.

One day in my sophomore year (1957) at Fairfield Prep I struck out 19 apprentice plumbers, bricklayers and carpenters from Bullard–Havens Technical High School. That night Johnny Barron, an aged Cincinnati bird dog, called at my house. When I answered the phone he asked to speak with my father and after that my mother, like some Victorian suitor seeking permission to court me— which in a way he was. Finally I took the receiver with trembling hands. His voice surprised me. It was battered and broken but completely at ease, as if he was talking to an old friend. And in his mind I guess we were old friends. Hadn't he just seen me pitch?

Johnny took much for granted as we talked. He detailed my strengths and weaknesses with a familiarity that would have annoyed me if not for the warmth in his voice. He concluded his little talk by saying, "And when you do

make the big leagues it will be your fastball that brings you there. It's a marvelous fastball."

It was a strange word to use, I thought, the kind of word one used in discussing a painting or statue or some other thing of beauty. He was a strange man, too, and I wondered how he knew such things. (As it turned out, he didn't.)

"We can't offer you a contract until you're a senior," he told me. "By that time most of the other clubs will be bidding a lot of money for you. I'll be out of the picture by then. Our scouts and front-office people will have taken over. But I hope you'll remember that I was the first scout to appreciate your gift. It will mean a lot to me."

Although I was not sure what he wanted or why, I promised, and he hung up, satisfied. I seldom pitched a game that year without spotting his face somewhere in the sparse crowds, and often I would not feel comfortable on the mound until I did. When I signed in 1959, however, it was with the Braves, not with the Reds. But I still kept my promise and had the local paper carry a small article saying how Johnny Barron Sr. of Haddon Street, Bridgeport, Conn., had been the first scout to get in touch with me.

After the bird dogs, came the full-time scouts. They moved in like carpetbaggers in your junior and senior years to take advantage of the friendships cultivated by the bird dogs. By that time the bird dogs had drifted out of your life, like first lovers who could not bear to see the others.

The scouts were younger men, usually in their 50s, and their appreciation for talent was more professional than esthetic. They were not unkind men, however, although they were certainly not so lovable as the bird dogs. But then again, when you got your first whiff of that big bonus cash, maybe you were not so lovable either. And just maybe it was a good thing that the bird dogs like Johnny Barron could not see you now.

Unlike the bird dogs, whose virtues were intrinsic to their natures, the scouts were men who embellished their natures. It wasn't that they created virtues they did not possess; it was just that they overaccentuated the virtues they had until they became caricatures of themselves.

Jeff Jones, for example, was "sincere." He was a large, egg-shaped New Englander with shrubs for eyebrows and an endearing stutter that could melt the hardest of hearts. Jeff did not toss his sincerity about like bruised fruit either; he deposited it where he knew it would do the most good —with the mother of a prospect.

"Why, Miz Jordan," he would say, "dddon't you worry about your bbboy! When he gggoes away to the minor leagues I'll watch over him as if he were mmmy own son."

And when Jeff did not look after you as well as he might have, it was understandable. Jeff Jones signed 15 sons a year and, after all, a father can only do so much.

Ray Garland was "flamboyant." He was a sharp, dapper little man who had long ago become a master of the grand gesture. To this day I can remember Ray in only one pose. He is standing, unprotected, in a heavy drizzle that has drenched his camel's hair overcoat the color of Gulden's Mustard. His left arm is extended away from his body, his hand clutching an umbrella that is over the head of my

4

mother, who is sitting dryly in her wicker chair, watching me pitch.

John Pollodoro was "enthusiastic." He was a little Italian with poorly fitted false teeth. When John got excited his teeth started clicking faster than the words could escape from his mouth and he looked like an actor in a poorly dubbed foreign movie whose image was out of joint with its sound. One day in my junior year I saw him sit next to my girl friend (now my wife) in the deserted stands of a West Haven ball park. He was jabbering away like a machine gun, but my girl was just nodding primly and moving down the bench away from him until finally she and he were wedged into the far corner of the stands. After the game she told me she had been frightened of him. "When he found out I was your girl friend he even offered me a job," she said. "I know what kind of job he was offering. My mother told me about such things."

I told her she was mistaken, that Johnny was just trying to find some way he could get to me through her. "Be nice," I said. "He could be buying our house someday."

And finally there was the scout I'll call Jack Brown. Jack had no essentially admirable qualities that he could exaggerate like the other scouts. He was just a likable, harmless old fellow whose face was so red it seemed always on the verge of spontaneous combustion. Jack was a drinker and often was in no condition to match wits with the sharper scouts, although maybe this worked to his advantage. Everyone felt sorry for him, and I'm not so sure he didn't sign more than a few players because of sympathy.

The Suitors of Spring

One day in my senior year Jack drove me to a tryout camp outside of Boston. We arrived the night before and took a motel room on the outskirts of town. I went to bed immediately, but he said he would sit up a few minutes. He sat nervously in a chair by the window, every so often glancing over at me to see if I was asleep. When he thought I was, he withdrew a paper bag from his coat pocket and began taking long swigs from it. I watched him through half-closed eyes until I fell asleep.

When all the scouting is done, when all the dinners, half-kindnesses, half-truths are in the past, the hard bargaining begins. The fight for the cash. The scouts are brushed aside now, just as the bird dogs were a few years before. The farm directors, general managers and vice-presidents take over. They are younger, colder, bread-faced businessmen who were once accountants or timekeepers. They seem unable to speak to you directly, even when you're in the same room with them. They always talk around you, to your parents, as if you were off on a long trip, maybe, or as if you did not really exist except as a talent somehow abstracted from the human being who possessed it.

But in the long run you never signed with a farm director or a vice-president or even the clubs they represented. In those days you signed a contract with a man, and the man was usually the scout who had made the deepest impression on you. It did not matter how insincere you felt their previous acts of kindness might have been, you could not entirely forget them. You knew even then that an the mound, since few adults bothered to watch the meaningless games your coach let you pitch as a sophomore, and because they always stood directly behind the home-plate screen, as if they would not feel comfortable unless viewing the world through a maze of wire triangles.

Few of the bird dogs ever got paid a cent for their efforts, although once in a while one would be promised a $100 bonus if the boy he touted ever made the major leagues. But even if that boy did make it, by the time he did the bird dog usually would have died. That wasn't why they went through the effort. They did it to pass time for one thing and because they loved the game for another—but most of all because they appreciated young talent. Just watching it develop was reward enough for old men.

One day in my sophomore year (1957) at Fairfield Prep I struck out 19 apprentice plumbers, bricklayers and carpenters from Bullard–Havens Technical High School. That night Johnny Barron, an aged Cincinnati bird dog, called at my house. When I answered the phone he asked to speak with my father and after that my mother, like some Victorian suitor seeking permission to court me— which in a way he was. Finally I took the receiver with trembling hands. His voice surprised me. It was battered and broken but completely at ease, as if he was talking to an old friend. And in his mind I guess we were old friends. Hadn't he just seen me pitch?

Johnny took much for granted as we talked. He detailed my strengths and weaknesses with a familiarity that would have annoyed me if not for the warmth in his voice. He concluded his little talk by saying, "And when you do

2

The Suitors of Spring

The bird dogs came first. They just appeared one spring day in your sophomore year of high school as if drawn by the odor of freshly cut outfield grass. On that day you knew for sure that your fastball, which had slowed considerably in the jump from a Little League to a high school mound, had once again begun to smoke like a burning pine. You knew also that your life would never be the same again. Baseball was no longer a game for you from that day forward. It was, instead, your career.

They were called bird dogs because they sniffed out talent, although the name does not do justice to the men. The bird dogs were kindly old men in plaid shirts and string ties. They owned taverns and hardware stores, and once had even played ball with Kiki Cuyler and Georgie Cutshaw. Now in their last years, they measured out the weekday afternoons at an endless succession of high school baseball games. They were always easy to spot, even from older man cannot spend two years of his life courting a boy without a little of himself rubbing off in the bargain, until even he is not so sure how much his original motives have been blurred and how much this boy really means to him. And you begin to wonder if maybe Jeff Jones did not really wish he could protect you at McCook and Davenport and Palatka and all those places you end up; and maybe Ray Garland would have held that umbrella for your mother even if you had been a .220-hitting second baseman; and maybe Jack Brown didn't want you to see him drink, not only because he wanted to sign you, but also because he wanted to protect you from a vice he thought you were too young to understand.

And if you never did make the big leagues, you did not feel badly that you let down the Braves or Yankees or some farm director. You felt badly because you had let down Jeff Jones or Ray Garland, as if your bonus money had been fished solely from their own shabby pockets.

I signed with Jeff Jones in 1959, when he was with the Braves; when I left baseball in 1962 because I lost my fastball, I seldom saw him or any of the other scouts again. Only Jack Brown used to pop up once in a while at a high school or American Legion game. I would see him behind home plate in the midst of a group of parents, rambling on in that indefinable drawl of his that could have been the faded remnants of a Southern past. And when his attention wandered from the action it invariably seemed to settle on his hatred of the free-agent draft. Jack did not really know how to hate, so when he came to the free-agent draft his tongue would knot in his mouth until he couldn't speak, just sputter. He hated the free-agent draft because, as he said, "It's taken all the heart out of scouting. It's made everything automatic and meaningless." And then he would fall sullen and silent.

It was difficult to see why Jack (and most of the other old-time scouts) hated something that made his job easier. The free-agent draft was initiated in 1965 to prevent the scouts and clubs from cutting each other's throats in bidding wars over untried youngsters. To eliminate such wars, the major leagues made all free agents eligible for two drafts each year, one in June, the other in January. If the boy did not sign with the club that drafted him, he went back into the pool for the next draft. The process repeated itself until he either signed with a club that had drafted him, enrolled in a four-year college, in which case he could no longer be drafted until he was graduated, or had passed 21 or was no longer drafted.

At no point, however, was the boy free to bargain with any club other than the one that had drafted him. This kept his bonus demands within reason. The only thing the clubs had to do was make sure their offers were just tempting enough to convince a boy it was foolish to waste six months of his career until the next draft, especially since the second club might offer him an even smaller bonus than the first. Now, instead of prospects pulling in $175,000 bonuses like Rick Reichardt, the No. 1 pick in the country was lucky to get $70,000, and the fourth and fifth picks struggled to grab $30,000.

Jack Brown and the other scouts hated the draft not because they no longer had to spend large sums of money but because it made their occupations half-obsolete. Before the draft a scout's job consisted of evaluating talent (it did not take much insight to know a fastball that sounds like ripping silk is big-league stuff) and convincing (*i.e.,* conning) the prospect to sign with the scout's club. If teams offered the prospect roughly the same bonus, what made him pick one team over another? It was usually a scout and the impression he'd made on a boy. But that's exactly what had become obsolete.

"It no longer mattered if the kid and his parents loved me," said Brown. "If we didn't draft him he couldn't sign with us no matter what."

I never understood just how much scouting—and maybe baseball—had lost because of the free-agent draft until I drove to Stamford, Conn., one day to watch an 18-year-old Stamford Catholic High School pitcher named Art De-Filippis. A husky left-hander with thick arms, DeFilippis had a smooth sidearm motion and a fastball that behaved like a screwball. In four years of pitching he had won 35 games, lost 2, struck out 451 batters in 248⅓ innings and allowed only 13 earned runs. *The Sporting News* ranked him as one of the top 12 prospects in the country, which made it likely he would be drafted in the first round. (He was eventually drafted second by the Washington Senators, which made him the 38th pick.)

It was not hard to spot Art DeFilippis' father on that hot May afternoon as his son took the mound against Xavier High School of Middletown in a state tournament game. He was sitting in an aluminum deck chair on a high rise that runs above the first-base line. A rugged-looking, olive-skinned man with a thin gray mustache, he had a long green cigar clenched between his teeth. His pretty blonde daughter sat beside him, looking a little confused, as if not quite sure what to make of this fuss over her younger brother. Every so often she would look up and smile at the many friends who stooped to whisper in her father's ear. Their question was always the same. "Any news from the scouts?"

"What do I know?" said Mr. DeFilippis in disgust. "I see them at every game. I say hello and they don't even say a word to me. Look at them!" he said, gesturing with his cigar to the 16 or 17 older men clustered behind the home-plate screen. He said something in Italian and his friends laughed. His daughter watched the game as if she had not heard a thing.

Someone brought Mr. DeFilippis the latest *Sporting News* with the story about his son. He read the article carefully, nodding, and then he showed it to his friends. He slapped the paper with the back of his hand and said, "See, what'd I tell ya?" The friends nodded solemnly.

It was only the scouts who did not come over and whisper in Mr. DeFilippis' ear. They sat in deck chairs or stood in small clusters. Although many of them were strangers to me, they did not look so different from the old men I had known 10 years ago. They were still tanned and weatherbeaten from their long Florida springs, while we in New England were just beginning to turn red on these first few warm days, and they still dressed a little flamboyantly for older men, in bright alpaca sweaters and ban-

lon jerseys and white and black tasseled loafers. Some
smoked cigars, a few chewed tobacco and only a handful,
it seemed, kept careful notation of the game's progress in
their little black notebooks. They looked much more relaxed, convivial, than I ever remembered scouts being.
Scouts were nervous, frantic men before the free-agent
draft, always trying to figure some way to outsmart their
cohorts in latching onto a prospect. Now they looked as if
buzzing in Art DeFilippis' ear was the farthest thing from
their minds.

I walked over and sat on the hill behind home plate, a
few feet beneath the scouts. They were talking about good
restaurants nearby and their next stops and old friends
they hadn't seen in a long while, and none of them seemed
to concentrate very much on the game. But then again, it
was a boring game. Art DeFilippis had already fanned
eight of nine batters with a fastball that was tailing and
sinking when thrown low and rising when thrown high.
He had a nice loose motion, and I could tell he loved
pitching just by the way he savored every moment he was
on the mound. He must have been pitching a long time,
since Little League at least, because he knew when to turn
his back on a batter, when to throw over to first base to
hold a runner and when to look for a ball's rough spots
after it had been fouled off. Only once in a while, however,
did any of the scouts comment on him. Often they even
had to ask one another how he'd gotten that last batter out,
because they'd missed it.

In the fourth inning DeFilippis hit an inside-the-park

11

home run. "He hits, too?" asked a heavyset, white-haired man in his 60s who sat down beside me.

"I guess," I said. He asked the other questions about DeFilippis (What kind of boy was he? Did he like the game? Was he interested in signing?), and we talked for a while, only half-watching the game, until finally he introduced himself as Paul Florence, a Houston scout. Ten years ago, I told him, he had scouted me when I was in high school. He said he remembered, although I'm not sure he did because he kept calling me Bob after that.

"Who did you finally sign with?" he asked.

"Jeff Jones," I said. "He was with the Braves then."

"Ah, Jeff," he said, smiling and nodding with satisfaction. "I'll bet Jeff romanced the hell outta you in those days, didn't he?"

"As a matter of fact, he did. Aren't you doing the same with the kid?" I asked, pointing toward the mound.

"No, it's not necessary anymore. Not after the draft. If it wasn't for the draft I'd be romancing his whole family, maybe take them all to dinner tonight and invite them down to Houston. But that would be foolish. I'd just be getting his hopes up, and mine, for nothing if we didn't get to draft him. All I do is watch him pitch a few times, write up a report on him and turn it in. The front office decides what to do about him after that."

Art fanned his eleventh of 12 batters in the fourth inning, and I could see his father clapping politely as he left the mound. Paul Florence continued talking.

"You didn't romance the kid just to get at him, either, you know. The thing was, the more time you spent with him the more you learned what he had inside. What made him tick. You couldn't measure that just by watching him pitch. You had to know the boy for that. Now, with the draft, you seldom get to know any of the boys you scout. They're just names." He stopped for a minute, then added, "It's all so depersonalized. There's no excitement, enthusiasm in it anymore. No life—you know what I mean?" He looked at me, a little confused, as if even he were not so sure he knew what he was trying to say. "You know what I mean?" he asked again.

The innings drifted by and as the seventh was about to begin, Paul stood up. "There's no sense staying any longer," he said. He shook my hand, said goodby and then added, "It's a shame, a real shame."

"What is?"

"It isn't only baseball, you know. Everything's depersonalized. No one cares about the people they deal with anymore, not the waiters or department store clerks or anybody. Did you ever see those smiles you get from the stewardesses on an airplane? It scares me to death, the way when they turn around those smiles disappear."

Paul Florence left and so did most of the scouts. One who remained was Bob Clements, a tanned man in his mid-50s. Clements was formerly a Pittsburgh scout but is now the assistant director of the Major League Scouting Bureau. The bureau, organized in 1968 and run by Vedie Himsl, a former Cub executive, offers freelance scouting services for a fee to all the major league clubs. Although not all clubs have availed themselves of its services, it seems just a matter of time.

13

"We owe our existence to the free-agent draft," Clements said. "Before the draft, clubs spent a fortune scouting a kid. One year Kansas City spent over $600,000 in bonuses, and that's not even including what it cost to keep 30 to 40 scouts on the payroll. If a club liked a kid enough they'd move a scout right into his town for a few years so the scout would get in the kid's good graces. And then they had to spend $100,000 to sign him anyway. I wouldn't give an 18-year-old kid $100,000 if he could self-levitate."

Clements turned to a scout next to him and asked how DeFilippis got that last out. "Strikeout," said the scout, and Clements marked it in his notebook.

"Things have calmed down a lot," he continued. "The draft has eliminated all the special treatment the big prospects used to get. Now they're all the same to us. There's no distinction. And because it's no longer necessary for a scout to get personally involved with a boy, you don't need as many scouts. That's where we come in. We offer to scout kids and turn in reports on them to all the clubs. It beats duplication of effort. Then all the clubs have to do is send a scout to see the kid in his senior year and they make up their mind how high they want to draft him. They can cut a lot of deadwood off their payrolls that way. Instead of 3 to 40 scouts they'll need only six or eight."

I asked him if eliminating scouts wasn't just another step toward depersonalization of baseball.

"We're not the cause of that," he said, as if personally hurt by the accusation. "The free-agent draft did that. We're just filling a need that came up. Why, before the draft all those old-timers were complaining how tough it was trying to sign a kid. Now they're complaining it's no longer fun. I don't believe any of them. I bet you won't find one in 40 who would rather go back to the way things were before the draft—except, of course, those whose jobs we'll replace."

"Then you think baseball is a lot better off because of the draft and your organization?" I said.

He looked up quickly. "No, I didn't say that. I never said things were better or worse. I just said this is the way things are, that's all. And there's nothing that can be done about it. You have to learn to live with it."

It was the ninth inning now. Clements stood up, folded his chair, tucked it under his arm and said goodby. He was the last scout to leave. Even the fans along the first-base line were beginning to fold up their blankets and chairs in anticipation of the last out. Art DeFilippis had already fanned 20 batters, and one more would be a new career high for him. Mr. DeFilippis looked worried about his son, who was exhausted after all those strikeouts and the inside-the-park home run. As I walked past, I could hear him talking.

"I don't know who he'll sign with," he was saying, "but whoever it is, they'll have to meet our price. That's our only consideration now. I got a call this morning from a New York organization called Pro Scouts. They want to be Artie's agent for 10 percent. Maybe I'll let them do the dealing for us. Who knows? And if nobody comes up with the cash, Artie can go to college on a scholarship and then step into my business when he gets out. He can make

$20,000 a year with no problem, so why should he sign a contract for nothing, huh? Why?"

Art DeFilippis fanned his twenty-first batter, and his players mobbed him, as did the remaining fans. He didn't seem to notice that there were no scouts around now, until I mentioned it to him.

"When I was younger," he said, "I always heard stories about how the scouts took you to dinner and all. Every kid does. But none of that's happened to me. I've hardly said a word to them."

Most of the people had gone by now. I started walking across the Stamford Catholic football field toward my car, then heard a voice call out my name. I turned around to see Jeff Jones walking toward me, a huge grin on his bushy-browed face. He didn't seem to have aged at all in the 10 years. When he stuck out his hand I hesitated for a moment, remembering all that bonus money he had sunk into me, and I felt that I should make some explanation or apology to him.

"I thought it was you," he said, and began talking as if we hadn't seen each other in a few days and he was eager to catch up on lost news. He asked about my parents. He said he'd always liked them, especially my mother. At first I thought it was strange he said nothing about my wife and kids, until I remembered, of course, he didn't know about them.

I asked him why he wasn't out to dinner with the De-Filippis boy right now, and he said he never did that anymore. "It used to be fun competing with the scouts, but now what difference does it make?" Then he added, prod-

16

ding me lightly with his elbow, "And I was good at it, wasn't I?" I noticed he didn't stutter as much as he used to. "You know, I could never understand why you didn't make the big leagues," he said. "I thought for sure you would. What happened in the minors?"

"It was just one of those things," I said. "You remember, Jeff." He nodded, but I'm sure he didn't.

"Yes, that's the way things turn out. Well, I hope you saved all that bonus money. You didn't waste it, did you?"

I told him I bought a house with it, and he nodded his head in approval.

"Good, good, I'm glad you got something out of it. I always like to see my boys do well, even if they don't make the big leagues for old Jeff." We had reached the parking lot. "What are you doing now?" he asked.

"I write," I said.

"Oh, I see. So that's why your hair is so long," he said. "That's all right. It's the style today. But you must remember never to let it go to extremes. You must never go to extremes, Pat," he said with a stern look. It was the same kind of look I remember the day I left for the minor leagues and he told me I must never do anything to embarrass him, because now I was one of "Jeff's boys." He had again fallen into that half-sincere, half-created tone that he had used so often with me and a thousand other boys 10 years ago.

"I'm writing a book, too," I said. "It's about baseball in the minors."

"I hope you included old Jeff in the book," he said. And when I said yes, I had, and looked away from him, it must

17

have occurred to him that I had written something that might not have shown him in his best light.

"You treated old Jeff right in that book, didn't you?" he said, and he put his arm on my shoulder. "I sure hope you did right by me, Pat. You know I always liked you. I had a special interest in you. . . ."

"Like a father would a son?" I said.

"Yes, that's it," he said. "Like a father would a son."

And just for a moment that old charlatan had me believing he always did have a special interest in me, and I felt suddenly close to him and Jack Brown and Ray Garland and all those other old men, and I thought, damn it, Artie DeFilippis will never even know what he's missed.

The Living Legend

Stephen Louis Dalkowski, a pitcher, signed a minor league baseball contract with Kingsport, Tenn., of the Class D Appalachian League shortly after his eighteenth birthday in 1957. He was given his unconditional release by San Jose, Calif., of the Class C California League shortly before his twenty-seventh birthday in 1966. In nine years of professional baseball, mostly in Class D and C towns like Kingsport and San Jose, Pensacola, Fla., and Aberdeen, S.D., Dalkowski won a total of 46 games, lost 80 and fashioned a lifetime 5.67 earned-run average. His best won-lost record was 8–4 with Stockton, Calif., in the California League in 1964. However, throughout much of his career, which covered 11 teams and nine leagues, Dalkowski managed records like 1–8 with an 8.13 ERA at Kingsport; 0–4 with a 12.96 ERA at Pensacola; 7–15 with a 5.14 ERA at Stockton; and 3–12 with an 8.39 ERA at Tri-Cities. Dalkowski never pitched an inning in the major leagues, and pitched only 24 inn-

19

ings as high as Triple A, where his record was 2–3 with a 7–12 ERA.

On May 7, 1966, shortly after his release from baseball, *The Sporting News* carried a blurred, seven-year-old photograph of Dalkowski, along with a brief story headlined LIVING LEGEND RELEASED. The first sentence of that story read as follows: "Steve Dalkowski, a baseball legend in his own time, apparently has thrown his last professional pitch." The story was not considered particularly dramatic at the time since few people even on the periphery of organized baseball had not heard of Steve Dalkowski.

To understand how Dalkowski, a chunky little man with thick glasses and a perpetually dazed expression, became a "legend in his own time," it is necessary to go back 10 years to a hot spring day in Miami, Fla. Dalkowski is pitching batting practice for the Baltimore Orioles while Ted Williams watches curiously from behind the batting cage. After a few minutes Williams picks up a bat and steps into the cage. Reporters and players, who had been watching with only casual interest, move quickly around the cage to watch this classic confrontation. Williams takes three level, disciplined practice swings, cocks his bat and then motions with his head for Dalkowski to deliver the ball. Dalkowski goes into his spare pump. His right leg rises a few inches off the ground. His left arm pulls back and then flicks out from the side of his body like an attacking cobra. There is a sharp crack as his wrist snaps the ball toward the plate. Then silence. The ball does not rip through the air like most fastballs, but seems to just reappear silently in the catcher's glove as if it had somehow decomposed and then recomposed itself without anyone having followed its progress.

The catcher holds the ball for a few seconds. It is just a few inches under Williams' chin. Williams looks back at the ball, then out at Dalkowski, who is squinting at him. Then he drops his bat and steps out of the cage.

The writers immediately ask Williams how fast Steve Dalkowski really is. Williams, whose eyes were said to be so sharp that he could count the stitches on a baseball as it rotated toward the plate, says that he did not see the pitch, and that Steve Dalkowski is the fastest pitcher he ever faced and probably who ever lived, and that he would be damned if he would ever face him again if he could help it.

Ted Williams was not the only baseball authority who claimed Dalkowski was the fastest pitcher of all time. Paul Richards, Harry Brecheen, Earl Weaver and just about anyone who had ever seen the New Britain, Conn., native throw, claimed he was faster than Feller and Johnson and any of the fabled old-timers. The Orioles, who owned Dalkowski from 1957 to 1965, sent him to the Aberdeen Proving Grounds in 1958 to have Army equipment test the speed of his fastball. The fastest pitcher ever evaluated by such equipment was Bob Feller, whose fastball was clocked at 98.6 mph. On the day Dalkowski threw into the machine, his fastball was clocked at 93.5 mph. But Feller had thrown his fastball from a high mound that added 5 to 8 mph to its speed; Dalkowski had thrown from level ground since there was no mound available. Also, Dalkowski had pitched a game the day before, and that alone would have accounted for at least a 5 to 10 mph loss in speed. And finally, Dalkowski was literally exhausted by the time the machine clocked his fastball because he had to pitch for 40 minutes before he had thrown a fastball within range of the machine's measuring device. All things considered, it was conservatively assumed that Dalkowski's fastball, when right, traveled at well over 105 mph, truly faster than that of anyone who ever lived.

But it was precisely his wildness, almost as much as his speed, that made Dalkowski "a legend in his own time" and eventually prevented him from ever reaching the majors. In nine years of minor league pitching he walked 1354 batters in 995 innings. He struck out 1396. In his last year of high school Dalkowski pitched a no-hitter in which he walked 18 batters and fanned the same number. In 1957 at Kingsport, he led the Appalachian League with 129 walks, 39 wild pitches and 121 strikeouts in 62 innings. He once walked 21 batters in a Northern League game, and in another contest he struck out 21 batters—both league records. In 1960 Dalkowski set a California League record by granting 262 walks in 170 innings. He fanned the same number. In 1961 he set a Northwest League record of 196 walks in 103 innings while striking out 150 batters.

Stories of Dalkowski's speed and wildness would pass from one minor league town to another, each player picking them up, embellishing them and passing them on, as if by the mere act of embellishing he was in a sense sharing in those feats. There was the story of the hapless batter whose ear was torn off by a Dalkowski fastball; or the home-plate umpire who was knocked unconscious for 30 minutes by a Dalkowski fastball; or the outfield fence that was splintered by a Dalkowski fastball thrown on a bet; or the brick wall demolished; or the home-plate screen ripped to shreds, scattering all the fans and convincing them to never again sit behind home plate when Steve Dalkowski pitched. And then there was the Williams' story. Players who knew of Dalkowski always ended with the Williams' story, as if that was the one supreme compliment to his talent.

Inevitably the stories outgrew the man until it was no longer possible to distinguish fact from fiction. But no matter how exaggerated the stories might have become, the fact still remained that Dalkowski struck out and walked more batters per nine-inning game than any other professional pitcher. There was also considerable proof that he was the fastest hurler who ever lived. And it was because of his blinding speed that the Baltimore Orioles put up with him through eight years of little or no success. Every spring the Orioles' management would conduct a new experiment with Dalkowski in an attempt to discipline his talent. They made him throw fastballs at a wooden target. They made him throw on the sidelines until exhausted, under the assumption that once his lively arm was tired and his speed was muted slightly it would be easier for him to throw strikes. They bought him thick Captain Video-type glasses to correct his faulty 20-80, 20-60 vision. They made him pitch batting practice every day for two straight weeks in the hope that facing a batter would help guide his pitches. And finally they made him throw only 15 feet away from his catcher, believing that once he threw strikes from that distance, the distance could be gradually increased to 60 feet, 6 inches, from where he would also throw strikes.

After twenty minutes of throwing at a wooden target the target was in splinters. No matter how long he threw on the sidelines his arm never got tired. His thick glasses only served to further terrify already terrified batters. No matter how long he pitched batting practice he still had trouble throwing the ball inside the cage, let alone over the plate. And after two weeks of throwing at a distance of only 15 feet, Dalkowski could still no more throw a strike from that distance than he could from 60 feet, 6 inches.

In the end, all the experiments failed. There were a number of reasons, not the least of which was the fact that if ever a man was truly possessed by his talent it was Stephen Louis Dalkowski.

"When I signed Steve in 1957," said Baltimore scout Frank McGowan, "he was a shy, introverted kid with absolutely no confidence in himself. Even in high school he was so wild he would walk the ball park. But we gave him a $4000 bonus, which was the limit at the time, because Harry Brecheen said he had the best arm he ever saw. It's possible, too, that Paul Richards might have given Steve a little something under the table because he was so anxious to get hold of him. Everyone knew it was a gamble, he was so wild, but we all thought he was worth it. Now that Steve's out of baseball I feel there were three things in particular that prevented him from making the big leagues. The first was that boy he almost killed in Kingsport. He hit him on the side of the head with a fastball and the boy never played ball again. They say he was never quite right in the head after that, either.

"Following that incident Steve was always terrified of hitting somebody. One year Clyde King, his manager at Rochester, put a batter on each side of the plate and made Steve throw to them both simultaneously. He threw five of six strikes right down the middle, possibly because he knew that if he threw the ball either left or right it would hit one of them.

"Another reason he didn't make it was that he was too easily led. He seemed always to be looking for someone to follow, and in the minors he followed the wrong guys. He was never a bad kid, really, but he liked to drink a little, and raise hell at night, which certainly never helped his career. One year I remember we sent him to Pensacola to play under Lou Fitzgerald, an easy-going old-timer. And who do you think Steve got hooked up with down there? Bo Belinsky and Steve Barber. That had to be the three fastest, wildest left-handers any manager had to cope with—both on the field and off. Yet I think Steve could have made it if he was ever led by the right guys. Once we put Harry Brecheen behind the mound to talk to him on every pitch. Steve threw nothing but strikes. But the minute Harry walked off, Steve was as wild as ever.

"And finally I think the Orioles made too much of a fuss over Steve in his early years. They were always billing him as the 'fastest pitcher alive,' and I think the publicity hurt him. Stuff like taking him to the Aberdeen Proving

Grounds and conducting all those experiments. I think he would have been a lot better off if they had just left him alone in the minors and let him move up by himself. . . . But even that might not have done it, I guess. What it all boiled down to was the fact that Steve never made the major leagues because he never did learn to control Steve Dalkowski—period."

But if he failed to discipline himself and his talent, Dalkowski made a herculean effort. He never took exception to the many experiments the Orioles' performed with him, even though at times he doubted them. Brecheen once said that if ever a man deserved to make the major leagues it was Dalkowski, "because of the determined way he went at pitching and the cooperation he always showed in those long hours of work."

Many people close to Dalkowski felt he suffered those experiments too good-naturedly, that he should have gotten angry and rebelled against them. But rather than become angry with all the interest in him, he seemed bewildered and confused by it. No matter how many hours he worked in the distant bullpens of Aberdeen and Kingsport and Pensacola, Dalkowski never really seemed a part of the experiments. He always gave the impression that he viewed them from outside himself, as if they were being conducted not on him personally but on a body that belonged only partly to him and partly to a lot of other people who had a stake in him.

Furthermore, people said, he never got angry enough for success. If he could only begrudge someone else their success, if he could only become mad at those with inferior talent who surpassed him, it might inspire him to succeed. But he said he never envied anyone else's success, and then added, "I never met a ballplayer I didn't like."

"No one ever wanted to succeed more than Steve," said Ken Cullum, a friend of Dalkowski's from New Britain. "He would run through a brick wall if he had to. But he always seemed afraid that his success would have to come at the expense of someone else. And he could never hurt anyone like that."

By 1962 the Orioles had tired of Dalkowski. The previous year they had come up with four young pitchers, Steve Barber, Chuck Estrada, Milt Pappas and Jack Fisher, who together had won 56 games, and now they no longer worried about Dalkowski's progress. He was shipped to Elmira of the Class A Eastern League, and immediately the front office began scanning their lower minor league rosters to see where they could ship him next once he became insufferable to manager Earl Weaver. But under Weaver, an intense, roly-poly little man, Dalkowski began to throw strikes—relatively speaking. For the first time in his career he walked fewer batters (114) than innings pitched (160), while still striking out a substantial number (192). He won 7 games, lost 10, and posted a respectable 3.04 ERA. He led the league in shutouts with 6, and he also completed 8 of 19 starts, the most of his career. The following spring with the Orioles at Miami, Dalkowski said Earl Weaver had given him confidence.

"I felt that Steve had been given every tip on control that was ever known," said Weaver. "I knew that the smartest pitching coaches in baseball had worked with him. There wasn't anything I could tell him that he hadn't heard a hundred times before. The one thing I did try to do was keep quiet."

During the spring of 1963 Dalkowski's progress was the talk of the Orioles' training camp. In a two-inning relief stint against the Dodgers he fanned five and gave up no hits or walks. Harry Brecheen said that Dalkowski was just the short reliever the Orioles had been looking for, and then added: "The boy has come a long way. There is no doubt of his improvement. He is more settled as an individual and he deserves to make it. Steve is a good kid."

Toward the end of spring training Dalkowski was interviewed by a reporter who asked him if all the strenuous activity he had placed on his arm had ever damaged it through the years. Dalkowski admitted that he had lost a little off his fastball at the age of 23, but then said, no, he had never really had a sore arm in his life. A few days later in an exhibition game, Dalkowski fielded a bunt and threw off-balance to first base. He got the runner, but also pinched a muscle in his elbow. He was never the same pitcher again.

The Orioles shipped him to Rochester of the International League, hoping that his arm might come around. But he pitched only 12 innings there, then 29 innings at Elmira. For the first time in his career he was unable to average one strikeout per inning. The following season he started at Elmira and then drifted down to Stockton, where he was 8–4 with a 2.83 ERA. His arm apparently had begun to heal, but he hurt it again in 1965 and was sent to Tri-Cities of the Class B Northwest League. In

1961 he had fanned 150 batters in 103 innings at Tri-
Cities; in 1965 he managed only 62 strikeouts in 84 in-
nings, the worst record of his career. In mid-season the
Orioles released him, and he was picked up by the Los
Angeles Angels and sent to San Jose. The following spring
the Angels gave him his unconditional release.

Today, five years after he left baseball, Dalkowski's name
still evokes recognition from anyone who ever participated
in professional baseball. Recently Dick Schaap, the noted
sportswriter, asked Tom Seaver to name the fastest pitcher
ever. Seaver did not hesitate in answering "Steve Dalkowski," although he added he had never seen him pitch.

But Steve Dalkowski's real fame rests not with the Tom
Seavers in cities such as New York. Instead, it lies in all
those low minor league towns like Wellsville and Lees-
burg and Yakima and Stockton, or wherever talented but
erratic young players are struggling toward the major
leagues. To these minor-leaguers Dalkowski will always
symbolize every frustration and elation they have ever felt
because of their God-given talent. They take pride in re-
calling his successes, as if his was the ultimate talent, and
his struggle to discipline it, the ultimate struggle. If Steve
Dalkowski had succeeded it would have given proof to
their own future success. But even his failure does not
diminish him, for it was not the result of deficiency but
of excess. He was too fast. His ball moved too much. His
talent was superhuman. To young players he is proof that
failure is not always due to a dearth of physical talent. So,
in a way, Dalkowski's lack of achievement softens the possibility of their own imminent failures.

Dalkowski could only have succeeded if he had tempered his blazing speed with control and discipline—in short, had compromised his fastball, because with control inevitably comes a loss of speed. His wildness can be considered a refusal to give up any of his speed, even in the hope of gaining control and big-league glory. Instead, Dalkowski settled for those isolated, pure, distilled moments of private success attributable solely to talent. And those moments could never be dimmed, because their purity was inherent in his talent. That he never won a major league game, never became a star, is not important to young ballplayers who hold him in such reverence. All that matters is that once, just once, Steve Dalkowski threw a fastball so hard that Ted Williams never even saw it. No one else can claim that.

An Old Hand with a Prospect

Woody Huyke, smiling, blows Bazooka bubbles as he walks with quick pigeon-toed steps away from home plate. His shin guards click between his legs and his chest protector rises and falls against his chest as he moves. His gray flannel uniform is darkened with sweat. His cap is still on backwards, and his oval, olive-skinned face is streaked with red dirt and sweat and the lighter outline of his mask, which he carries tucked under his left armpit. Two swollen fingers, taped together, stick out from the fat, round catcher's mitt on his left hand.

When Woody Huyke reaches the visiting team's dugout he turns slightly to shake the hand of a tall, impassive Negro who has just walked in from the pitcher's mound. Woody says something in Spanish and Silvano Quezada smiles. The rest of the Waterbury Pirates' baseball team arrive simultaneously from their positions, and they in turn slap Huyke and Quezada on the back before disappearing into the dugout.

31

A voice from the dugout calls out, "Nice going, you old goat." Both Huyke and Quezada smile. The remark could have been directed at either of the two men, who claim to represent the oldest living battery in the Eastern League. Together they have played 25 years of minor league baseball. Their combined ages is somewhere near 70. "That's 70 years that are known," Huyke will say with a raised eyebrow. "God only knows how old Quezada is. He is ageless. Me, I am a mere boy in comparison." Soon Woody Huyke will be 34.

Before Huyke disappears into the dugout he pauses on the top step, rests his elbows on the tar-paper roof and scans the Elmira, N.Y., ball park. It is a chipped and sagging wooden structure with a high tier of roofed stands rising directly behind home plate and lower exposed stands lining each foul line. The outfield, which is nothing more than intermittent clumps of grass, is bordered by a high wooden fence painted with the faded advertisements of banks and gas stations and restaurants.

On this hot, muggy July afternoon there are less than 100 fans scattered throughout the ball park. The largest group consists of seven or eight heavily made-up young women seated directly behind the home-plate screen. These are the wives of the Elmira baseball players. Throughout the game they have chattered amiably, like colorful magpies, and now that it is over they seem not even to have noticed, for they are still chattering. Woody looks at the girls and the few old men sleeping high in the shade of the home-plate stands and the young boys fooling in the third-base bleachers and he shakes his head. Then he steps backward onto the field and, still facing the empty stands, says with just a trace of a Spanish accent, "Thank you, ladies and gentlemen. Thank you for your wonderful applause." And he bows. It is the graceful and profuse bow of a conquering matador. He pulls off his cap with a flourish and sweeps it across his chest as he bows so deeply from the waist that his face almost touches the ground. And then Woody Huyke, too, disappears into the visiting team's dugout.

Woody Huyke is smiling because the Waterbury Pirates, a farm team of the Pittsburgh Pirates, have just won the first game of a twi-night doubleheader from the Elmira Royals, 1–0, behind Silvano Quezada's four-hit pitching. The victory has moved the Pirates into second place in the Double A Eastern League behind first-place Reading, Pa. If the Pirates ever hope to catch Reading they must also win today's second game before they leave tomorrow morning for a three-game series in Reading.

Just three hours earlier the Pirates had stepped off a Trailways bus after a six-hour ride from their home in Waterbury, Conn. They had had only enough time to change into their uniforms in the Mark Twain Hotel and wander conspicuously about town for a few minutes before reboarding the bus to the ball park.

The ride through the beautiful Hudson Valley had been both long and tiring, and it had made that first game victory only partially satisfying. A second victory would make it almost worthwhile. But not quite. It had been too tedious a trip ever to be worthwhile, opined one Waterbury player.

The Suitors of Spring

During the six-hour ride, which began at 9:30 in the morning, many of the players tried to sleep. They jacked their knees up into their stomachs, flattened their hands into knuckled pillows and closed their eyes to the pines and lakes that flashed before their windows. In between naps, many of the players drifted in and out of an endless, shifting game of pinochle that had been organized in the front of the bus by their manager, Red Davis. Before the ride would end, every player but two would be devoured by that pinochle game.

At 20 years old, Bruce Kison had no patience for pinochle; and at 6 feet, 5 inches tall, he had not experienced enough Trailways buses to be able to fold his frame into a cramped seat to sleep. Instead, Bruce passed much of his time glancing through a copy of *The Sporting News*. Bruce bypassed most of the stories about Tom Seaver and Sam McDowell, and turned instead to the back pages, where he scanned the many columns of statistics that told of the accomplishments of other minor-leaguers like himself. Bruce always looked first for news of other Pittsburgh farmhands, specifically pitchers, so that he could see just who stood in his way to Three Rivers Stadium.

Woody Huyke did not sleep or play pinochle either. He had been on too many 28-hour bus rides to be impressed by a mere six-hour jaunt, so he did not need to divert himself with cards or sleep to escape boredom. Nor did Woody read *The Sporting News*. He did not have to read of other Pittsburgh farmhands because there was no one, either beneath or above him, who could cause him anxiety. Instead, as was his custom, Woody talked ceaselessly to anyone who would listen, and finally, after three hours, he would talk only to himself. He spoke in a slurred, stammering English with only a slight Spanish accent. When he spoke his lips pulled up into his left cheek so that every word seemed punctuated by a wink.

Woody talked first about his 12 years in minor league baseball. He said that he had played organized baseball in three countries—the United States, Canada and Mexico—and not many players could claim that. Then, when he saw he was losing his audience, he began talking about his winters in Puerto Rico, where for three months of every year he played baseball with some of the most famous major-leaguers: Roberto Clemente, Frank Robinson, Orlando Cepeda—men he would not meet during the regular season because he had never played one inning of major league baseball.

"I caught some beautiful games in Puerto Rico," Woody said. "But the most beautiful game was in 1965 when I caught Louis Tiant against Juan Pizaro. That was when both still threw good. The game went 10 innings before Pizaro won 1–0." Huyke paused. "Ah . . . that was a beautiful game—you know what I mean? I would have paid to be a part of it." Woody turned in his seat and elbowed Ray Cordiero, a balding 32-year-old relief pitcher, who was trying to sleep. "Heh, Rook, you know what that means to catch such a game?" Cordiero grumbled an obscenity and turned toward the window. "Rookie!" said Woody in disgust.

After four hours of traveling the bus stopped at a roadside diner and the players got out to stretch their legs and eat lunch. When the journey resumed the players were still grumbling about the greasy food they had just eaten. Woody, who sat up front, immediately began smacking his lips and rubbing a flattened hand over his stomach. "That was a great meal, eh, Rook?" he said to Cordiero. The 11-year veteran looked sideways at Huyke and then said it was the greatest meal he'd ever eaten. Huyke nodded emphatically. "I loved it, too," he said. "I love it all." Then Woody turned in his seat and faced his grumbling teammates. "Heh, boys, this road trip is great, isn't it? Tell the truth, don't you love it as much as old Woody?" The players began to hoot and swear, and someone threw a rolled up *Sporting News* at him. "Bah!" said Woody, as he flung the back of his hand at his teammates. "These young kids, what do they know? Always complaining. They don't appreciate the finer things in life, eh, Rook?" He nudged Cordiero again. "What are they gonna do when they get our age, huh, curl up and die?"

Cordiero turned toward the window again and put his hands over his ears. "Why the hell don't you shut up, you old goat?"

Now, after catching the first game of the doubleheader, Woody Huyke sits in the shade of the Elmira dugout too tired to unbuckle his shin guards and chest protector. Steam rises from his face. It is a handsome, boyish face with full lips that make it look almost puffy. Woody has tanned skin, a heavy beard, warm brown eyes and shiney black hair that is beginning to recede from his forehead. He stands about 5-11 and weighs 195. At 33 years of age he is just beginning to be stocky, although he claims that his uniform size is the same as the one he wore as a 20-year-old rookie. What he does not admit, however, is that the uniform no longer fits him the same way. The buttons at his waist seem about to explode, and his pants fit his calves like an added layer of skin. But that is not entirely due to the refried rice and beans Woody loves so much. It is also due to the constant bending and standing a catcher suffers each game, which make his legs round and muscular like gigantic bottles of Coke. Woody worries a lot about his weight, although if he was in the majors he could afford the luxury of a few extra pounds. But as a minor-leaguer he knows that if he gains too much weight he will be out of a job.

Because of his age, Woody ordinarily wouldn't have to catch the second game of this doubleheader. Today is an exception. His backup catcher is on military reserve duty, and furthermore, Bruce Kison, the Pirates' talented young pitcher, will be making his first start in over two weeks after tearing a muscle in his right elbow.

A few minutes before the second game Cordiero returns to the dugout with a Coke and a hot dog for Woody. Woody eats slowly in the dugout and then goes down to the left-field line where Kison has already begun to warm up with one of the Waterbury utility players. Woody stands behind Kison and watches carefully as the young right-hander throws.

Bruce Kison's small, pink face is covered with "peach fuzz" which makes him look no older than 15, so his teammates have nicknamed him "Sweetie." Whenever they call him that in shrill, affected tones, with pinkies raised, Bruce will smile good-naturedly, although his face grows noticeably pinker and his eyes, which are a clear, almost cold blue, seem suddenly much too intense for such a baby-ish face.

His teammates have also called him "The Stick" at various times, because at 6-5 and 170 pounds he has the long limbs and small chest of a stick figure. His uniform shirt billows at the waist like a sail and his pants billow at the calf like harem pants. At no point does his body impose any definition on the uniform he is wearing. Because of his youthful face and awkward build, it seems incredulous that Bruce Kison is a superb, mature athlete. And yet, when he begins throwing a baseball in that easy, loose-limbed way of his, both his awkwardness and his innocence are dissipated and he looks proficient beyond his years.

Now, with Woody Huyke watching him, Kison is throwing much too hard and too rapidly after his layoff. The ball is dipping into the dirt and sailing over the head of his catcher, who must repeatedly run back to the left-field fence to retrieve it.

After each wild pitch Kison, whose face is expressionless, paws the dirt with his spikes only to throw even harder and more rapidly once the ball is returned to him. When he does throw, his arm sweeps out from the side of his body and crosses in front of his shirt waist-high, right to left. It is the same trajectory a bat takes when swung. When he finishes up, his arm rises noticeably, which makes his fastball go up and in to a right-handed hitter. ("A very tough pitch to hit," says Woody.) It is a fluid, sidearmed motion that appears to be effortless, and it is not unsimilar to that of other great sidearmed pitchers such as Don Drysdale and Ewell "The Whip" Blackwell. But like the motion of those pitchers, it often produces sore arms. When an overhand pitcher throws a curveball his elbow twists downward, its natural direction; a sidearmed pitcher twists his elbow upward, which puts great strain on muscles and tendons.

Two weeks ago Bruce Kison's meteoric rise from the Pirates' lowest minor league team in 1968 to its second highest team in 1970 was halted when he threw a curveball and strained an elbow muscle in his right arm. This was the first sore arm of Kison's career, and now, throwing in the Elmira bullpen, he is wondering if it will be his last. That is why he's throwing so hard so quickly. He wants to prove that his arm is no longer sore, and also punish the arm for having let him down for the first time in his life.

After Kison's sixth wild pitch his catcher looks up at Woody. Huyke nods and walks over and takes his catcher's mitt. Kison throws a low fastball that Woody expertly scoops out of the dirt. Before returning the ball to Kison, Woody says a few words to Kison's previous catcher. Kison waits for the ball. He takes a deep breath. Woody finally returns the ball to him, and Bruce immediately fires a fastball over the catcher's head. Woody gets up from his crouch and walks slowly back to the fence for the ball. He picks it up and walks back to the plate and returns the ball to Kison, who by this time has taken three deep breaths. The next pitch is a strike. Woody gets out of his crouch and walks a few feet toward Kison and shakes the ball at him, saying, "Atta boy, Bruce, use your head."

Before long Kison has calmed down considerably and is

throwing fastball after fastball into Woody's glove. Finally, Woody calls for a curveball. Bruce spins one up cautiously. Woody looks to see if he winces on it. He calls for another curve, and again Kison just spins it up softly. After a few more halfhearted curves Woody shrugs and goes back to calling for fastballs.

"I know how the kid feels," says Woody. "He's afraid to cut loose on the curve. He knows what a sore arm can mean to his career at this stage." Woody goes on to say that it is not the seriousness of this particular sore arm that is causing both the Pirates' front office and Bruce Kison any anxiety, but the feeling that this sore arm may be the beginning of an irreversible pattern that will follow Kison wherever he goes. Bruce knows if he is still to be considered a prospect he must prove he will not be a perpetually sore-armed pitcher. That's why today's game is so important to him. It will determine to a great extent when and if he ever makes the major leagues.

This game is also important to Woody Huyke, although not in the same way. Woody will never play in the major leagues no matter what. But if he can contribute in some small way to the development of a prospect like Bruce Kison, if he can guide him out of this sore arm by making sure he warms up properly, by calling the right pitches, by making Bruce twist his elbow a little less strenuously on a curveball, then maybe Woody Huyke will have a job in baseball after his playing days are over.

Elwood Bernard Huyke was born in Santurce, Puerto Rico, in 1937. He was raised in nearby Morovis, where his mother taught school for 41 years and his father worked for the government for 21 years. Although his father had played sandlot and college baseball, he had misgivings about his son going directly into professional baseball out of high school, so he convinced Woody to enroll at the College of Agricultural and Mechanical Arts in Mayagüez. After two years Woody transfered to Inter American University in San Germán where he became a biology major in the hope of someday becoming a doctor.

In his junior year in 1958 Woody was selected to compete in the Central American Games in Venezuela. He batted .408 in that tournament and attracted the attention of a number of major league scouts. He was eventually signed by Pete Zorrilla of the New York Giants to a $225-a-month contract. In the spring of 1959 Woody left school for spring training in the States, but before he left he promised his father that he would return the following fall to finish college.

After spring training Woody played only one month in Artesia, N.M., before the Giants' farm director, Fresco Thompson, told him he was being given his unconditional release.

"I begged him to find someplace for me to play," says Woody, "because I had already decided that baseball would be my career. He said there wasn't anyplace to send me. I pleaded with him every day for almost a week and finally, just to shut me up, he said okay, and sent me to Hastings, Nebr., of the Class D Rookie League."

Woody, who played third base at the time, hit well from his first day in Hastings, and his manager, Leo Schroll, started him every game. "Leo was a funny guy," says Woody. "He made all his players go to church on Sunday or else he'd fine them $25. But the minute he got on the baseball field he would swear left and right. At the time I didn't believe athletes drank beer, much less swore, so I thought it was terrible. One day he started swearing at me because I had made an error at third—I was a real butcher then—and I didn't think it was right so in front of all the guys I told him he shouldn't swear like that. It wasn't nice. He just looked at me as if he couldn't believe it. I still get a Christmas card from Leo and his wife, so I guess he didn't mind. She always signs it 'Ma.'"

In Hastings Woody lived at a hotel that charged a dollar a day for a bed and had a knotted rope out the window labeled "fire escape." Because the Hastings ball park had no facilities for the players to dress, Woody dressed in the hotel each day and walked two miles through town to the park. The first time he arrived at Elmira this year and discovered the same conditions he said, "I thought those days were behind me."

Woody was Hastings' best home-run hitter and eventually tied two other players for the league title with 12. During one stretch he hit five home runs in four days against the league-leading McCook Braves' pitching staff. He then went to Kearney where he hit a home run his first time up off a stocky right-handed pitcher named Jim Bouton.

"It was a knuckleball," says Woody. "Even then Jim was fooling with it. I never saw him again until 1966, and you know, even though he was a star he remembered me.

I didn't think he would. But still, I don't think he should have written that book of his. Baseball is an institution. Ballplayers have to protect it. For the good of the game you've got to omit some things."

Woody had the best hitting year of his minor league career in 1959. He batted .311 with 12 home runs and 50 RBI in only 62 games. He never again hit as many as 12 home runs despite the fact that he played in as many as 113 games a season.

"In 1959 I thought I could hit anyone," he says today. "I don't know what happened along the way, but 12 years later I don't hit so well. What am I hitting now, .230? A few weeks ago I was hitting good and then I hurt my shoulder. When I got back in a groove again I busted my finger. Now I don't feel good at the plate. But that's the way my whole career has gone, always injuries that have stopped me."

When Bruce Kison finishes his warm-ups, he and Huyke walk back to the dugout as the Elmira Royals take the field. Woody throws his arm around Bruce's shoulder and talks softly into his ear. Bruce nods. In the dugout Bruce dries his face with a towel and Woody gets a Darvon pill from his trainer and a fresh supply of Bazooka bubble gum. The bubble gum is to keep his mouth moist during the game, and the Darvon pill is to kill any pain he feels from a chronically sore arm. He has taken a Darvon pill every playing day of his life since 1964.

It is about 8 P.M. when Huyke trots out to catch Bruce Kison's first warm-up pitch in the bottom of the first inning. There is a loud click and the Elmira lights go on around the park. It is twilight and considerably cooler now. There are about 400 fans in the stands. Bruce, who towers on the high pitcher's mound, begins his warm-ups deliberately. Just as he throws his last pitch and Woody fires it down to second base, a woman behind the visitors' dugout says, "Look at that pitcher! He looks so young—like a little boy."

Bruce Kison was born in 1950 in Pasco, Wash. Pasco is one of the tri-cities of Pasco, Kennewick and Richland, which sit on the point where the Snake River empties into the Columbia. All three towns are rich farming communities, although there is also an Atomic Energy works that produces plutonium for nuclear reactors. Bruce's father dabbled a bit in farming, as did many Pasco families, but for most of his working years he sold hardware supplies. Bruce's relatives, however, were full-time farmers—wheat, alfalfa, corn, cattle—and each season Bruce worked on those farms as a boy.

"I hauled hay, cut cucumbers, picked tomatoes, everything," he says, "until I thought my back would break in two. I used to sweat something terrible in the sun. And all the while I was picking up and down the rows, I used to daydream about some day becoming a major league baseball player, just to keep my mind off the pain in my back."

When Bruce was ten years old he discovered that he could throw a baseball harder than most boys his age, so he switched permanently from the outfield to the pitcher's mound. "By the time I was 12 I had pitched several no-hitters in Little League—like a million other guys, I guess. In one game I struck out all 15 batters (a five-inning game) although there were a few hits sandwiched around those strikeouts. Ever since then the possibility that someday I might be able to pitch a 'Perfect Game' is always in the back of my mind when I take the mound. It's a game in which I strike out every batter I face on three straight pitches. But I guess that's every pitcher's dream, isn't it?"

Bruce had moderate success in such teen-age organizations as the Pony and Colt leagues, but it wasn't until 1966, when he played under Al Daniels at Pasco High School, that he showed any signs of becoming a professional prospect.

"At that time I was about 6-4 and 150 pounds," he says. "I was so awkward that I got cut from my high school basketball team, which had to be the first time any 6-4 kid got cut from basketball. I wasn't only awkward physically, but also mentally, and it was Daniels who toughened me up in both categories. Daniels was a former minor-leaguer who tried to run his high school team with the same toughness and discipline he would a pro team. Most of the players and parents thought the boys weren't ready for this. I personally thought it helped me a lot. For instance, once I had two strikes and no balls on a batter and Daniels told me to waste a pitch. I threw it down the middle and the batter hit a double. Daniels was furious and yanked me right out of the game. Sitting on the bench at the time, I didn't know what to make of it. But now, looking back, I realize Daniels taught me what I could expect from pro ball."

Bruce opened his senior year with successive no-hit games and finished with a third no-hitter. That summer of 1968 he was drafted (not very high) by the Pirates and was signed by scout Babe Barberis to what Bruce calls "a sizable bonus contract, although I'd rather not say exactly how much."

Before he would sign his contract, Bruce made sure the Pirates included a stipulation that allowed him to finish his spring semester in college each year before joining a minor league club in early June. At first the Pirates balked at such a deal, but finally they acquiesced under the assumption that any time they wanted Kison to drop out of school for a semester they could easily convince him it would be to his best interests. Before he left for his first assignment in the summer of 1968, Bruce enrolled at Columbia Basin Junior College for the fall term, although he eventually switched to Manatee Junior College in Bradenton, Fla., in the spring of 1969. This was done so he could participate in spring training while still attending college, since the Pirates trained at Bradenton.

"I wanted to make sure I got a chance to go to college," says Bruce. "You see so many guys who drop out for one reason or another. And what do they have left when their baseball days are done? Nothing! I'm determined that won't happen to me."

After signing, Bruce was immediately sent to Bradenton in the Rookie Gulf Coast League. "When I got there I couldn't believe how many guys were in Pittsburgh uniforms. There must have been a hundred. There were a lot of Spanish guys, too, the first I'd ever seen. They were always off together yakking away so that no one could understand them. It seemed that everyone belonged to some clique or other, except me. I was too shy to bother with anyone except my pitching coach, Harvey Haddix. There were 25 pitchers in camp and they were supposed to have only 12 by the end of the season. It was like a pressure cooker. It was always boiling hot and everyone was running around trying to cut each other's throat so as not to get released. You'd make friends with a guy one day and the next day he'd be gone. You'd begin to wonder when it would be your turn. After a few days down there I began to think I'd be cut. In a situation like that you grow up pretty quickly. You learn to evaluate yourself and your talent honestly, or else. In the end there were only 12 pitchers left. I was one of them."

Bruce pitched in 10 games at Bradenton, 9 of them in relief. He won 2, lost 1, posted a 2.25 ERA and managed nine strikeouts in 24 innings. He described his modest success simply by saying, "I got some people out. On the day I left for Pasco, Harvey Haddix came over to me and said I was one of the boys he considered a prospect. I said thanks, but on the way home I wondered if he didn't say that to a lot of guys. By the time I returned to Pasco I thought I was a real stud around town. I told everyone I was going to give baseball two, maybe three years, and then if I wasn't in the bigs I'd quit. But now I've already been in two years and I'm going to find it hard to quit if I'm in Double A or Triple A next year. I guess I'll stick it out a little longer, maybe five years. But I definitely won't stay in as long as Woody has. I can't understand how

47

a guy like him, with his intelligence and almost a college degree, can hang on like he does. If I'm not going anywhere in three more years I'll quit and go back home. I'll finish college and maybe become a teacher and a coach. This baseball is a nice game and all that, but not in the minor leagues. If I was in Woody's shoes I would have quit a long time ago and become a doctor. But I guess that isn't for me to say—everyone has to live his own life."

In early June 1969, after attending Manatee Junior College, Bruce was assigned to Geneva, N.Y., of the New York–Penn League. The Pirates had tried to get Bruce to drop out of college for a semester so he could report to Geneva at the beginning of the season in May. He refused. Bruce was 5–2 at Geneva, with a 3.16 ERA and 77 strikeouts in 94 innings. As he put on a little weight, 10 pounds, he began throwing much harder, so that by the spring of 1970 he was assigned to the Pirates' Class A team at Salem, Va., in the tough Carolina League. He was 3–1 with an .082 ERA after five games, and was promptly called up to Waterbury in June. When Bruce arrived in Waterbury he watched a few Eastern League games and then decided that it wasn't such a tough league after all. "Any good high school pitcher can win in this league," he said, "as long as he throws the ball over the plate." He proved he was as good as his word by pitching a two-hit shutout in his first start. He followed with another shutout against league-leading Reading (also a two-hitter), then lost a pair of close games, 3–0 and 3–2. He was 4–4, with a 2.25 ERA and 43 strikeouts in 60 innings, by the time he took the mound against Elmira.

48

"I wasn't the same pitcher at Waterbury I was at Geneva in 1969," he says. "At that time I was still worried about being released. One day my roommate, Steve McFarland, was let go, and it really shook me up. I thought he was a pretty fair ballplayer. But by the time I got to Waterbury things like that no longer bothered me. I knew I was beyond that stage. I'm established now, and all I have to worry about is my career and how soon I get to the majors. Harding Peterson, our farm director, told me a few days ago that I was one of the organization's top prospects. But you can't rely on that stuff. The front office never gives you too much information because they're afraid you might get the idea you're too good."

A few days before the Waterbury Pirates left for Elmira, Harding Peterson, a tanned, ruggedly handsome man who looks like a representative from a Billy Graham Crusade, arrived in Waterbury to look over his organization's talent. The night he arrived, Red Davis held a clubhouse meeting. He told his players that Mr. Peterson did not like to see his players come to the ball park in dungarees or Bermuda shorts. After the meeting Woody Huyke shook his head and said to Bruce Kison, "You gotta dress up for the man, you know." Kison looked at him and replied, "That's a lot of bush league crap."

Before the game that night, Peterson sat in the Waterbury dugout and watched the Pirates take batting practice. He wore a lime sportjacket, dark slacks and tasseled strollers. For long periods of time he sat motionless, his legs crossed, as he stared intently through dark glasses at the

49

players performing before his eyes. When he saw Bruce Kison he called him over, and for almost an hour the two men talked in muffled tones before Bruce finally returned to the outfield to shag fly balls.

"Bruce is definitely a prospect," says Peterson. "He just has to learn a few things. Three years ago we thought he was only a chance prospect, but he's gotten considerably faster since then. And he's not afraid to come tight on hitters like some kids are. We think so highly of Bruce that we moved him up in mid-season, something we rarely do. We prefer to let young pitchers build their confidence in the lower leagues. But Bruce already has it. He can handle any problems he'll encounter at Waterbury without getting shook. We have a lot of older pitchers at Pittsburgh and we'd like to get Bruce there as soon as possible. That's why I'm here today, to try to talk him into playing in the Winter League this year. He wants to go to college, though. I told him he can always go to college but that he has only about 20 good years to devote to baseball. But whenever we ask Bruce to do things like that he's always got a thousand and one questions for us: What good will it do me? What about my draft status? How much money will you pay? What about my college degree? He's a very well-organized boy. Other guys you can talk into doing things they don't really want to do. They'll stammer a lot and hesitate, but in the end you get them to do what you want. But not Bruce. He plans ahead."

When the Pirates were almost finished with batting practice, Peterson stepped out of the dugout, brushed the dust off his slacks and walked behind the batting cage to talk with different players. One of the last men he talked to was Woody Huyke. He asked Woody about certain players on the club, and which ones would play winter ball this year. Finally he asked about Bruce Kison's progress. The only man Peterson did not ask Woody Huyke about was himself.

"When we drafted Woody for $8000 from the Oakland system last year we had no thought that he was a major league prospect," says Peterson. "Even he knows he's no prospect, although I certainly wouldn't be embarrassed to use him in the majors defensively. We drafted Woody mainly because he's a fine, intelligent fellow with a good reputation for getting along with people. Woody is what's called 'an organization man.' His job is to work closely with the manager and front office in bringing kids like Kison along. And because of Woody's Latin background he serves as an excellent liaison man between the front office and Latin players. I know Woody's never made any real money in this game, so I told him that if things work out there might be a job for him in our system someday— maybe as a coach or manager. But I never promised him anything definite. It's too soon. We still have some use for him as a player. For example, we planned on using him at Columbus in the International League this year, but when Milt May came along faster than we expected we sent Woody to Waterbury. The conditions here aren't as good as at Columbus and some other players might have balked at going down after playing five years in Triple A. But we felt Woody knew what was expected of him; and he went. We believe Woody would go to our lowest minor league club if we asked him, even though he's already been that way 10 years ago."

Ten years ago, in 1960, Woody Huyke was drafted by the Kansas City Athletics, given a $450-a-month salary and assigned to Monterrey in the Mexican League. The first Monterrey road trip consisted of a 28-hour ride to Tulsa, Okla., on a dilapidated school bus. It was 110 degrees in the shade when the bus left Monterrey and it got hotter as the trip went on. The bus stopped only twice, and both times the players got out and bought watermelons. The team arrived in Tulsa at 7 A.M., but instead of going directly to the YMCA, where the club was staying, the manager ordered the driver to go to the ball park.

"The manager was really crazy," says Woody. "He was furious with us for losing our last game, 14–0, so he took us to the ball park and conducted a 7:30 A.M. workout to teach us a lesson. We didn't get to the YMCA until 11. We were supposed to get some sleep before leaving for the park again for a 7:30 P.M. game. When we got to the YMCA there weren't enough beds for us so we had to sleep on mattresses in the halls. It was 102 degrees inside with no fans or air-conditioners. People kept stepping over us all afternoon and looking down at us as if we were crazy. I lost eight pounds on that trip."

Despite all this, however, Woody hit well at Monterrey and was batting about .350 three days before the Mexican League All-Star game, in which he was to play, when he suffered the first of a series of injuries that would hamper his career for the next 10 years. "I broke my finger sliding into second base on a double. I went to the Monterrey Hospital after the game and they said it was fine. The owner of our club said there was no reason to pay for an X-ray and advised me to go home and soak it in hot water. At 4 A.M. the finger was throbbing so bad I thought it would fall off. When I went to the owner next morning he said, 'Exercise it and it'll be okay.' I argued with him for 20 minutes before he finally agreed to have it x-rayed. The X-ray showed the finger was broken after all. At the hospital the doctor said he had no anesthesia so he would need two nurses to hold me while he straightened it. I said, 'Don't worry, I'm a tough guy,' just to impress the nurses, who were very pretty. Naturally, when the doctor touched the finger I fainted. When I woke up he had put a cast on it and told me I wouldn't be able to play for eight weeks. The Monterrey owner, who was not too happy over the hospital bill he had to pay, said that was fine with him but he wasn't going to pay me for not playing. When the Kansas City farm director found out about it he told the owner to send me to an American doctor in Shreveport, La. The owner didn't like that idea, either, so he bought me a bus ticket. It was a 12-hour bus ride and I refused to go. I said I wanted to fly to Shreveport. I knew, at the time, why the owner was giving me such a hard time. When I first got to Monterrey he had been very nice to me, letting me use his car whenever I wanted. Then I found out that he was a queer, and after that I wouldn't have anything to do with him. He got furious with me and now he was getting even."

In 1961 Woody was given $525-a-month and sent to

Shreveport of the Double A Southern Association. He was batting .307 and his fielding was just beginning to be respectable when he was sent down to Portsmouth, Va., of the Class A Sally League. "That hit me real hard," says Woody. "I thought I would make the All-Star team at Shreveport. I was leading my team in average, doubles and RBIs. I later found out that the Kansas City farm director had signed a kid he wanted to play at Shreveport. My manager said he had tried to prevent it but he couldn't. He said I was a real good prospect and should make the big leagues except for the fact I didn't have anyone behind me pushing me."

Despite his despondency Woody batted .307 with 43 RBIs in only 68 games. By the end of the season he had regained his enthusiasm to the point where he couldn't wait to start the 1962 season, one he felt sure would be his biggest ever. But in the fall of 1961 he was drafted into the Army, and in the spring he was driving tanks instead of baseballs.

The following spring (1963) Woody was invited to the Kansas City major league camp, along with another Latin prospect, Bert Campaneris. In three weeks there Woody got into only one ball game, against the Dodgers. He went 3 for 4 against Sandy Koufax and Don Drysdale. "I was so scared with all those big-leaguers around that I never went out of my hotel room, but when it came to hitting that was another story. I had all the confidence in the world. I didn't give a damn who was pitching. I felt I could hit them. It was the confidence of being young, I guess. I didn't know any better."

When Woody was finally sent to the Kansas City minor league camp, the first thing his new manager, Clyde Klutz, did was convert him into a catcher. "I hated it," says Woody. "All day long they fired baseballs from a bazooka at my shins. I was all bruises but I was too afraid to complain. I was afraid they'd send me home if I did. After a few weeks Klutz bought me a catcher's glove and told me how I had a much better chance to make the majors as a catcher. When I realized he was right, I actually began to enjoy it."

Woody was supposed to go with Klutz to Binghamton of the Class A Eastern League, but on the last day of spring training he was sent instead to Lewiston, Oreg., of the Class B Northwest League. Again Woody threatened to quit and go back to college, but Klutz and Hank Peters, the team's farm director, talked him out of it. They said it would be better for him to be a starting catcher at Lewiston rather than a second-string catcher at Binghamton. The next day Woody and five other Spanish ballplayers boarded a train for the three-day ride to Lewiston.

"In Minot, N.D., we saw our first snow," he says. "We got out and began throwing snowballs at each other while all the passengers stared at us as if we were crazy. When I got to Lewistown I lived with this old man, Roy Miles, who had dogs, cats and parakeets all loose in the house. Every night there was a different animal in my bed. I liked Roy, though, and made friends with a lot of other people in Lewiston. I used to have Sunday dinner at a different house each week, and I still get letters and cards from people out there. That's the way I've always been, I guess, easy to get along with, especially with fans."

Woody batted .317 at Lewiston, although he was near the bottom in fielding percentage for catchers. By mid-season, however, his fielding picked up and he was recalled to Binghamton. He was handed a plane ticket and told to fly directly to Charleston, W.Va., to meet the team. He was almost delirious with joy.

"It seems like just a little thing, flying," he says. "But by then I had taken so many trains and buses that I felt the organization had no interest in me, that they didn't consider me a worthy enough prospect to waste a plane ticket on. Now that they wanted me to fly I felt they must care something."

Woody caught his first game with Binghamton and his toe was broken by a batter's foul tip in the tenth inning. When Woody returned to the lineup a month later he hit two home runs in one game, but the next day he caught a foul tip off his throwing hand and broke his little finger. He was through for the season.

"I was going to return to college that fall," says Woody, "but Hank Peters asked me to go to the Winter Instructional League in Tampa. I said I'd rather go to college, but he said that this might be my big chance, that maybe next year I'd get a shot at the majors. I believed him because I always believed farm directors had the best interests of the players at heart. My mother had written a letter asking me to go back to college and become a doctor. But I ignored her and I went to Tampa instead. As it turned out, Peters was right. It was the turning point of my career, only not how he said it would be."

In one of the early Winter League games Woody attempted to throw out a runner at third base and felt something snap in his arm. The pain was unbearable, but he took a couple of Darvon pills between innings and continued to play. Although the pain disappeared temporarily, the next morning his throwing arm had turned purplish and was swollen twice its normal size. Woody rested three days and then played.

"I was ashamed to tell my manager I was hurt again," he says. "I had been hurt so often. But after a few weeks I couldn't even throw the ball back to the pitcher. They found out about it and sent me home. I went to 14 different doctors in Puerto Rico and each one said there was nothing he could do, the inflammation would be there for the rest of my life. In the spring of '64 the pain was not so bad, although the arm was still swollen, so I went to another doctor in the States. He said he thought I had cancer. I almost jumped out of my skin—I thought he was going to cut off the arm. After that I never again told anyone about the arm. I learned to live with it."

Despite his bad arm Woody was given $750 a month and sent to Dallas of the Triple A Pacific Coast League in 1964. His contract called for him to remain there at least 30 days before he could be shipped out. But after only one week, in which he went 2 for 7 in two games, Woody was told he was needed at Birmingham, Ala., of the Double A Southern Association.

"I couldn't understand why they wanted me there," he

57

says. "But Peters asked me to go so I went. When I got there I found out why. They wanted me to room with Bert Campaneris and a few other Spanish and colored players who were finding life very rough down South. Because I was white and could speak both English and Spanish, Peters felt I could make life easier for those guys. They even gave me more money than most players get in that league. Ever since then I've roomed with the colored or Spanish guys. At first it didn't dawn on me what was happening, and then gradually I began to realize I was no longer a prospect. They were using me as an organization man, although I still felt I was a prospect. But what I felt and what I knew was true were two different things. And the irony is, I had a good year at Birmingham. I batted .289 with 10 home runs. But I still couldn't throw the ball. It was embarrassing to have runners steal second every time they got on first. Sometimes I wouldn't even throw to second, because when I did the ball took three hops to get there and the fans would laugh at me. It was terrible for my pride, and after awhile I wanted to go hide.

"It got so bad that ever since that season I've been too ashamed to ask the front office for a raise, no matter what I hit. I've always felt I owed them for just keeping me each year. I mean, why should they have kept me? I was 27 and they had decided I would never play in the majors. I knew that. It didn't matter that I still thought I was a prospect. It had been decided. The only use I had to the organization was as an organization man. Now, I realize this was an honor, really. They were complimenting me by telling me I had other talents besides hitting and fielding. When you get old your hitting and fielding go, but the things I could do would never leave me. Not everyone can become an organization man. Lots of guys don't have the right temperament. They worry too much about their batting average and such. They're not smart enough to adapt, to change their thinking, to forget about their own success. You have to be a certain type of guy to be an organization man, and it makes me feel good to know I'm that kind of person. But at Birmingham in 1964 I wasn't so sure that's what I wanted. I thought there was no sense playing baseball if you have no chance of making the majors. I often wonder today why I didn't quit right then and there. But for some reason I didn't. Maybe I still thought I could make them change their minds. Foolish!

"I'm glad I didn't quit. I love baseball too much to do anything else. When the season is over I'm grouchy all the time. I feel miserable. I'm always sick. I get imaginary pains, like a baby. Only when spring training comes around and I can put the uniform back on do the pains go away. Sure, I would have liked to play in the majors, but I still get fulfillment out of just going to the ball park, any ball park, every day, and putting on a uniform. I always arrive three hours before a game and get into my uniform right away. I feel at home at the park, and my uniform is like a pair of pajamas. When I have it on I relax just as if I was home in front of a fireplace with a pipe and slippers. To be like this I guess you have to be born this way, huh?"

After Bruce Kison completes his warm-up pitches Woody throws the ball to second and then walks to the mound to talk to Bruce. He tells Bruce that at the first sign of

pain he should speak up. Bruce nods, although he is thinking to himself that he won't say a word unless the pain
becomes unbearable. Woody pats him on the rear end and
jogs back to home plate. The opposing batter hands Woody
his mask (he has played against Woody for three years
now) and Woody says something to him. Both the batter
and the umpire laugh as Woody picks up a handful of dirt
and tosses it into the air. The wind is blowing slightly
from right to left. Woody waves his outfielders over a
shade, taps his metal cup to make sure it's in place, then
crouches behind the plate. Bruce gets the sign and throws
his first pitch. A strike. Woody returns the ball, and Bruce
looks quickly for the next sign and fires another fastball
for a strike. After two more wasted fastballs, Bruce strikes
out the first batter with his fourth pitch, a fastball.

On the pitcher's mound Bruce Kison does not look so
young or awkward anymore. His face shows neither anger
over a bad pitch nor satisfaction at a good one. His pitching motion, which has neither the baroque trappings of
one who is trying to hide deficiencies nor the barrenness
of one whose motion has missing vital parts, is spare and
quick. It is distilled of impurities, and so he has neither
to slow nor vary its workings. He throws each pitch from
the same sidearmed angle, with the same speed of delivery,
and with the same amount of time between each pitch. He
puts his foot on the rubber, gets his sign, delivers the ball,
then waits in his follow-through until Woody returns the
ball. Then Bruce turns, takes two steps back to the rubber,
turns again, places his foot on the rubber and waits for the
next sign. There is no wasted motion. He seldom rubs up

a baseball or removes his cap to wipe off imaginary sweat or turns dramatically to contemplate the center-field flagpole. Nor does he grit his teeth, shake his head in disgust or kick the dirt with his spikes as he was doing only moments before in the bullpen. He seems to have no self-conscious desire to call attention to himself, as do most young pitchers; nor does he stop his rhythm to regroup his thoughts after a setback. He is too modest for the former, too well-organized for the latter.

Bruce works his second batter to a full count before the batter lines out to center field. Although Bruce is as expressionless and mechanical as ever, he's obviously worried about his arm. No longer is he throwing as hard and recklessly as he was in the bullpen. And now, whenever Woody calls for a curveball, Bruce shakes him off.

"I've never had a sore arm in my life," says Kison. "When I hurt it two weeks ago I couldn't understand what had happened. There was a big knot in my elbow, and every time I moved my arm a certain way the elbow popped. I was more confused than worried at the time. I didn't tell anyone about it during the game, although I think Woody knew because he kept asking me how my arm was. I said it was fine and finished the game, which I won. I went to the doctor a few days later and he said not to pitch for a few weeks. I didn't tell anyone and took my next turn as usual. I walked about eight guys in three innings that game and Red came out to the mound and wanted to know why the hell I wan't throwing any curveballs. When I told him I had a sore arm he got real upset and pulled me right out. I could see why he was so worried, though. He's afraid if he lets anything happen to me it'll affect his career—which it would. If I was an older pitcher, an organization man like Quezada or Cordiero, say, then Red could take any chance he wanted with me and no one would care. Guys like Cordiero and Quezada don't have a chance to get a sore arm. That must be pretty discouraging to them, knowing that I'd get preferential treatment even though they might be as good as I am. I don't care what they say about loving the game and all that crap. It must be kind of hopeless playing every day knowing you have no real future as a player. I don't know whether I could stand it. That's why if my sore arm doesn't come around right away I think I'll quit."

When Bruce retires his third batter on another well-hit ball to center field, he immediately walks off the mound. He takes long, determined strides that carry him into the dugout before any of the other Waterbury players arrive from their positions. Red Davis, who was smoking on the top step of the dugout, leaps onto the field just as Kison arrives and walks quickly to Woody Huyke, who is waiting for him by home plate. Davis and Huyke confer for a few seconds, and Woody can be heard saying, "I think it's still sore, Red." Davis' head bobs up and down nervously and then he trots out to his third-base coaching box.

John Humphrey (Red) Davis was born 55 years ago in Laurel, Pa. Since he began playing professional baseball, at the age of 20, he has lived in over 25 U.S. cities, not to mention the few foreign countries, such as India, where he served in the Air Force during the war years of 1942–45.

Presently he lists his home as The Hotel Jefferson in Dallas, Texas.

Red is gaunt-looking, with the slack, mottled skin and excessively sharp features of a man who has lost too much weight too quickly. His once bright red hair and blue eyes are now faded, and his thin fingers are permanently stained with the nicotine of a thousand doubleheaders. After 35 years in professional baseball, of which only 21 games were spent in the majors, Red Davis has acquired an assortment of twitches and gestures that give him the appearance not of a former athlete but of some anxiety-ridden drummer who has stopped too often in Greenville and Mayfield and Corpus Christi.

The year 1970 marked Red's twenty-fourth consecutive season as a minor league manager. He has managed in leagues as low as the Class D Kitty League and as high as the Triple A International League, and yet his front office has never given him complete authority over certain of the players he was managing. His year at Waterbury was no exception. And Bruce Kison was one such player.

A few days before the Pirates were to leave for Elmira, Red decided to pitch Kison in his team's last home game. When Harding Peterson found out he immediately told Red it would be best to give Bruce a few extra days rest. Even though his team was fighting for a pennant, Red was perfectly willing to comply.

"Bruce is a fragile piece of property," says Red, "and I sure as hell wouldn't want to be the one to ruin his career. If he gets hurt it'll be my fault for not holding him back longer. If Bruce was an organization man I could take a

63

chance on him. That's their job, to play when hurt. An organization man knows that will impress the front office in case a coaching or managing job comes up in the future. Often that's the only reason they have a job in the first place, because we can do things with them we'd never think of doing with a prospect. This makes it easier on them, too, in a way. An organization man doesn't have to worry about his batting average or his ERA. He's not getting paid for those things. For instance, if Huyke is hitting only .230, it doesn't bother him that much because he knows he can help the team in other, less obvious ways, like keeping the guys in good spirits or helping Bruce along. Now, if a prospect was hitting .230, he'd be useless. He'd be worrying so much about his average that it would affect his fielding and base running, and eventually he'd hurt the whole team. The only thing that really matters to a prospect is his own success. But that's understandable, too, because that's all the front office judges him on. An organization man is evaluated by how much he helps the team. If he has any kind of personal success, that's it. That's why an organization man takes the pressure off a manager while a prospect puts it on him. I'd as soon have eight organization men in the lineup anyday. Most of the time they're better players, too, which makes you wonder why they never made the major leagues. Maybe they never got the breaks or didn't have anyone behind them. Who knows? Hell, that's been my problem, too. I should have been in the majors by now, as a coach or manager or something. I'd sure as hell rather be there than where I am. But there are some things you can't explain, I guess."

An Old Hand with a Prospect

Red Davis began his playing career as an infielder with Greensburg of the Pennsylvania State League in 1935. Like so many ballplayers during the late Thirties, he worked his way to the major leagues in the early Forties only to be drafted and serve his best playing years overseas. When he returned to the States in 1945, he was 30 years old and no longer a prospect. Red played for three more years as an organization man with Dallas of the Texas League before he finally decided to become a minor league manager in 1948. That same year he married Estelle Nicholas of Fort Worth, a girl he had met during his playing days. After their marriage they moved to over 15 cities, from Portland, Oreg., to Waterbury, Conn., while waiting for him to be offered the major league job that never came. Like so many baseball wives, Mrs. Davis absorbed so much baseball during those 21 years that she finds it impossible today to stray far in her conversation from talk of her husband's profession.

On the night of Waterbury's last home game before the trip to Elmira, Estelle Nicholas Davis, a skittish little woman with a high puff of white hair, stood in the darkened runway under the stands and waited for her husband to emerge from the locker room after the game. The ball park had emptied quickly of its 300 or so fans, and now, at close to midnight, only a few scouts and the wives of some of the players remained. Mrs. Davis smiled at three of these women, who stood off by themselves, and they returned her greeting. Then she continued her conversation with a tall, tweedy man named Buddy Kerr.

"Oh, yes," she was saying in a high, Blanche DuBois

voice, "I root for all of Red's old boys. I've always rooted for Willie McCovey and little Marichal ever since Red had them. But Marichal is having such a bad year, isn't he? I feel so bad for him."

Kerr stooped over and said something to Mrs. Davis and she smiled.

"Oh, the hip's coming along just fine. You know, I had this terrible accident last year. But it's coming along fine. I certainly wouldn't let a little thing like that stop me, now, would I? I'm still the same as ever. By the way, did you notice the crowd tonight? Do you think they'll draw here? I do hope they draw or else they'll have to pack up and move elsewhere."

A few minutes later, when her husband emerged from the locker room, Estelle Davis took his arm, said good-night to Buddy Kerr and the three wives, and left the ball park.

Of the three remaining wives, one was a heavily made-up blonde clutching a gray toy poodle; another was a well-built brunette in a lavender pants suit; and the third was a slender, athletic-looking girl in a plain green dress. The blonde and the brunette were in their early 20s and the athletic-looking girl was close to 30, although she actually looked younger than the others because of her short, boy-ish haircut and because she wore little makeup to mar her fine, straight features. The blonde and the brunette were talking animatedly to each other about the poodle, which they both referred to as "Baby" and which seemed quite used to being the topic of conversation. The girl in the green dress, however, said little. She stood slightly apart from the others, and only smiled faintly now and then, as if she, too, was used to her role—the third party in a two-party conversation—and not only did it not cause her any anxiety, but was actually much to her preference. Three years ago the girl in the green dress had become Mrs. Elwood Bernard Huyke, and in that span of time she had adjusted nicely to being the wife of a perennial minor league baseball player.

When Woody Huyke finally decided to get married at the age of 30, he wondered whether he would ever be able to find a "proper baseball wife" such as Estelle Davis. "A baseball wife is very important to an organization man's career," says Woody. "She can make life miserable for him if she's always nagging him to quit. That's why I waited so long. But it worked out all right. I've even saved a little money in the two years I've been married, which was more than I ever did when I was single. My wife and I are very compatible, really. She knows I'm impossible to live with when I'm not playing baseball, so she encourages me to play. That's one of the reasons I married her. Really, it is! I knew I would stay in baseball for the rest of my life, and I had to find someone who loved the game and could stand the traveling. I explained to her before we were married that baseball was everything to me. She accepted that. For example, one night a few weeks ago she had very bad pains in her chest. I took her to the hospital right away because I know she isn't the kind of woman to complain. I stayed with her all night and most of the next day until around 6 P.M. She didn't mind when I left. She knew I had

67

to be at the park for that night's game. I have never missed a game in my life, except for injuries."

Ann Marie Keckler Huyke always knew she'd marry an athlete, even when she was 13 years old and combining wheat on her father's farm in Gardner, N.D. Because Gardner was a town of only about 100 people, and there was very little to do with her free time, Ann Marie gravitated to sports, as did most other girls and boys in the area. She was tall and slim even then, so it was only natural that she turned to basketball, where she competed on equal terms with some of the boys. Ann Marie played basketball all through grammar school and high school, and in her senior year led the girls' team with a 21-point-per-game average. (She still plays basketball, and had a chance to compete with the Puerto Rican girls' team in the Pan-American games last winter.)

"Our high school girls' team had won the State Championship in 1955, '56 and '58," she says, "although we didn't win it my senior year, 1960. It's funny, but the boys' teams never did win a state title that I can remember. They never could produce, I guess. When I was in high school, though, I always dated athletes and was sure even then that I'd marry someone athletically inclined. After I graduated I went to Fargo Interstate Business College for two years and then got a job as a bank teller in Fargo, N.D. The only fellow I ever dated who wasn't an athlete was an actor from Fargo. I went out with him for about six months, just to see what it was like. But no matter how hard I tried I could never really enjoy the so-called "intellectual talk" of his set. To be honest, I couldn't understand it at all, and I often wondered if they really understood it themselves."

In 1966 Ann Marie and a girlfriend took their first "real" vacation away from home. They left in December for Puerto Rico, and since both were sports enthusiasts, the first thing they did on arrival at San Juan was to board a bus for an hour ride to Arecibo to watch a Winter League baseball game.

"I met Woody at that game," says Ann, "and although we didn't see each other too often during the next few years, we got to know each other through our letters, and were finally married in Fargo on Friday, Sept. 13, 1968. I had been a bank teller for six years, five months and three days before I quit to become a "baseball wife." Since then I've become an expert at boxing our belongings in a matter of hours for a trip to a new town. But I don't mind the traveling much. I actually like to see different parts of the country after living in Fargo and Gardner most of my life. And I think I get along well with the new people we meet at each town. I admit, though, that I still carry a picture of the house I'd like to settle down in someday.

"I can't complain. I've never had any visions of Woody playing in the major leagues, so I have nothing to be disappointed about. I knew what he was when I married him. He made that perfectly clear before he even proposed. But sometimes it's a difficult thing to explain to people who don't understand. I mean, some of the younger wives, wives of prospects, are always making comments about when *their* husbands get to Pittsburgh they'll do this or that, or *they* just couldn't stand these little minor league

69

towns if it wasn't for the fact that their husbands will some-day play in Pittsburgh. And then what can I say? You hate to have people think you don't have any faith in your husband just because you know he'll never make the major leagues. But you have to salt your feelings and prejudices with an honest evaluation of what he is. People are always asking me what he's going to do when he quits baseball. 'Is he going back to college to become a doctor?' they say. I know what they're hinting at, but I don't say anything. I just give them this blank look, as if to say I don't have the faintest idea what he's going to do. Even if I told them, they would never understand the positions in baseball open to a man like Woody. Or those he could have had outside of baseball that he's turned down. I would like to say to them, 'Look, my husband could have been a doctor if he wanted to, but he gave it all up to play baseball. This is what he loves. It's his job, and one day he's just going to fade into another position in baseball and that's all there is to it.' But I never do."

Often Ann Marie Huyke will come early to Waterbury Stadium with her husband. While he dresses in his uniform, she will pick a good, lightweight bat and step into the batting cage where a Waterbury bat boy will pitch to her for an hour. She has a smooth swing, not at all like a woman's, and from a distance she looks like a slim, long-limbed young boy in Bermuda shorts, not like a 27-year-old woman. Ann Marie will stay in the batting cage, hitting sharp line drives, until her husband emerges from the locker room. Then she will sit and talk with him on the grassy slope behind the cage before she goes back to their apartment, changes into a dress or a skirt and blouse, and returns to the stadium to sit with the wives of the prospects.

In the bottom of the second inning against Elmira, Bruce Kison loads the bases. He walks the first batter on four pitches and retires the next two easily. But the fourth hitter of the inning lines a single to center field. The hit comes off a slow, hanging curveball that Bruce visibly pulled back on. After the pitch Woody walks halfway out to the mound and yells at Bruce to "put something on the damn ball." Red Davis has again moved to the top step of the dugout. He says something to Woody as he gets down in his crouch for the next batter. "I think so," says Woody. Red turns immediately to the left-field bullpen and signals for Ray Cordiero to begin warming up.

Bruce bears down on the next batter, throwing all fastballs, and gets him to hit an easy grounder to the second baseman. Bruce takes a step off the mound as the second baseman fields the ball, then stops as the ball rolls off the second baseman's glove, up his chest and falls back into the dirt. Bruce returns to the mound, takes the second baseman's throw and turns immediately to get his next sign from Woody. He works the next batter to two strikes and one ball, then breaks off a hard, sharp curveball that retires the batter on an infield fly. It is Bruce's first decent curve of the night, and as he walks off the mound he is smiling faintly.

In the third inning Bruce gets two outs on fastballs and one on a hard curve. It is obvious now that he is gaining more confidence with each pitch. In the fourth inning of the scoreless game Kison cuts loose and strikes out all three batters. He is throwing considerably harder now, mixing almost an equal number of fastballs and curves on each batter. Following each strike Woody bounces out of his crouch, fires the ball back to Bruce and shouts encouragement. After the third strikeout Woody walks briskly away from the plate with a broad smile on his face. "That kid is throwing some kinda heat," he says to no one in particular.

Unlike the other players, Woody does not go into the dugout but sits instead on a small chair beside the dugout, as is his custom. It is somewhat cooler now in the top of the fifth inning, and Woody wraps his hand in a towel. "My fingers get numb," he says, holding up his throwing hand. The fingers are fat and discolored. They have been broken so many times that the circulation is poor and they get numb if Woody doesn't keep them warm.

Woody seems only partially occupied with the 0–0 game in progress. He turns often to talk with the different fans behind him, and he seems particularly amused by a very fat woman in a flowered dress, with whom he has been carrying on a dialogue every half inning. The woman, who is sitting with two equally obese friends, has stacked 10 empty beer cups on the dugout roof in front of her.

"Heh, cutie, talk to me some more," the woman says to Woody, and she smiles at him. It is a lopsided little smile that twists up into her cheek. Woody looks over at her and shakes his head. "You're a cute one," she says again, as she elbows one of her friends. "Isn't he cute, Martha?"

Woody shakes his head and laughs. "You know, you remind me of Buddy Hackett. Really! So help me God, doesn't she look like Buddy Hackett?" he says to all the fans around him. Everyone laughs at this, including the woman herself. Just as the last Waterbury batter of the inning is retired, the woman reaches across her friends and offers Woody a sip of her beer. But he doesn't notice her gesture. He is too busy yelling at Richie Zisk, the Waterbury batter, who has just flung his bat in disgust after striking out. Woody is yelling at Zisk not to die out there, and to hustle out to his position and shake it off.

"It's part of my job to be nice to fans," says Woody. "When you become an organization man that's one of the things you get paid for, bringing people into the ball park. If they like you, they come to see you play. When I was young, like Bruce, I was too embarrassed to talk to fans, but once I decided to be an organization man I had to learn a lot of new things. For instance, when I went to spring training with Kansas City in 1965 I knew my job was just to warm up pitchers and catch batting practice, but I did it with enthusiasm. It began to feel good knowing there were always little jobs I could do to help a team, even if I no longer got a chance to win ball games with hits. I liked the idea, too, that I might be able to help someone else make the big leagues, like Bert Campaneris, for instance."

From 1965 to 1970 Woody Huyke was a bullpen catcher first for Vancouver of the Pacific Coast League and then Columbus of the International League. He only played in about half his team's games each year, except by then it didn't matter so much. He had reorganized his entire thinking as to what he should be as a baseball player.

"I thought I could learn to be a good organization man if I dedicated myself to every aspect of the game of baseball," he says. "I no longer worried about my average or throwing arm, but concentrated on a lot of details other players don't ever bother with. I stayed away from bad publicity. I never said a bad word about anyone. I tried to instill the right attitude in other guys. I was nice to the fans. And whenever I did play, I made sure I always ran 90 feet. I became a real pro, and now I can proudly say that I always do what is expected of me. I can be counted on for certain things that many players can't. I'm always in shape. I leave parties before 1 A.M., instead of staying until 4:30. When I go to bed I'm always thinking of tomorrow's game: who's pitching, what kind of hitters he'll face, what kind of park it is. I try to plan everything now. I even make a joke of being the old man on the club so young pitchers, like Bruce, will have confidence in me."

Woody opened the 1970 season as a bullpen catcher for Columbus, but when a young prospect named Milt May progressed faster than expected, Columbus was stuck with two bullpen catchers. One night Woody sat down with his wife and discussed his prospects at Columbus.

"I told her that I was going to be sent down," he says. "It had to be me. There was no one else they could send. I couldn't blind myself to reality. I thought about my value to the organization and what I would do in their place and I decided they could use me best at Waterbury. A few days later I was told I was being sent to Waterbury.

It made me feel good, actually, to know that I understood my situation so well after all these years. When I was young I never felt I understood some of the things that happened to me. I was always too anxious about my career. But now I know where I am, and where I'm going, and what I have to do to get there. It makes life easier. I have no anxiety over things. At first when I realized I was going to be shipped out of Columbus I was a little upset because the conditions were very nice there. But you can always make yourself find things wrong if you know how. I don't like to fly anymore, and at Columbus we flew all the time. I knew at Waterbury the team traveled by bus. I convinced myself it would be much better taking a bus. See! It's easy if you're used to it. The only complaint I have about Waterbury is that some of the conditions are not so hot—like the lights at Pawtucket. You can get damaged for life or ruin a career playing under bad lights. As you get older you have to be aware of such things. Your body can't recover from injuries like it used to. When you're young who worries about playing conditions? You let your ability carry you. And if you are a prospect and you get hurt, the organization babies you. If you're an organization man and you get hurt, maybe you don't have a job anymore."

Bruce Kison retires the side in the fifth inning, but in the sixth he gives up two singles after getting one man out. Now, with runners on first and third and the score still tied 0–0, he knows he is in trouble. He gets the fourth batter of the inning to fly out to third base, and then he

75

fires two quick strikes past the potential third out. Woody crouches behind the right-handed batter and sticks out two fingers beneath his glove. Kison flicks his glove fingers to indicate he wants a new signal. Woody responds with a single finger and Kison nods slightly. Woody then hunches over the outside corner of the plate, but before he can set his target Kison flicks his glove again. Woody shifts himself to the inside corner of the plate and puts his glove at a level with the batter's knees. Again Kison flicks his glove. Woody raises his target until it rests just inches from the batter's chin. Kison goes into his motion and fires a fastball directly at the spot where the batter's head would have been if he had not fallen to the dirt. The count is now 1 and 2.

"When I want to knock a batter down," says Kison, "I have to do it myself. Woody doesn't like to call for knock-down pitches. He's afraid I might hit someone. Jeez, I hit eight batters in one game and it didn't bother me any. And we won the game. But it bothers him. I guess he's played against a lot of these guys and he doesn't want to hurt them. I can't afford to feel like that or I'll never get any-where. I think, too, Woody's conscious of injuries because he's getting older. That's surprised me about guys like him. I'd always thought they'd be tough, but they're more afraid to slide into second with their spikes up than the younger guys. Maybe it's because they know what an in-jury can mean to a guy's career. I just think that's a heck of a way to play the game—always worried. That's the trouble with a lot of these organization guys, they've lost their confidence over the years. They're always looking to play it safe. But how can you expect to get anywhere that way? You've got to take chances.

"They even let the front office push them around because they're afraid to speak up. I don't think I could take that. When Mr. Peterson tried to pressure me into going to the Winter League I told him I heard it was a waste of time. I've been playing ball since January and my body needs a rest. I want to go home and hunt geese and duck and go to school and have a little fun for a while. That might not sound important to some people but it is to me, so that's what I'm going to do. I need school, too, if I ever expect to get anywhere. I admit it doesn't interest me much now, but it's something that has to be done. For a lot of our guys it's too late for anything but baseball. But there are three or four different directions my life can take outside of baseball, and I want to make sure I keep those possibilities open."

With the bases still loaded and the count 1 and 2 on the batter, Woody Huyke flashes two fingers to Bruce Kison. Bruce flicks his glove and Woody immediately counters with a single finger. Bruce nods. Woody moves to the outside corner of the plate, but again Bruce flicks his glove. Woody straightens up slightly and moves back to the inside corner where he again places his glove underneath the batter's chin. Bruce throws and again the batter, hunched slightly forward expecting a curveball, hits the dirt. This time he does not get up so quickly, but looks back at Huyke and then out at Kison as if confused about something, as if some unwritten rule has just been broken and he wasn't informed.

Now with two strikes and two balls on the batter Bruce goes into his motion. The ball again is headed for the batter's body, waist-high, and the batter jerks slightly away from the plate as the ball breaks sharply in the opposite direction over the outside corner. It is a called third strike. The batter stands there flat-footed as Woody rolls the ball out to the pitcher's mound, which has just been speedily vacated by Bruce Kison. As Woody jogs back to his chair he is shaking his head and saying, "That Bruce is tough. Man, he's too tough for me!

"You know, I like that kid," says Woody. "He's got guts and confidence, like I used to have. When he's on that mound he battles your ass all the way. See the way he walks, head up, like he's ten feet tall! He's not afraid of anyone. He only gets bad when a couple of guys get hits off him. He doesn't think anyone should ever hit him. I tell him not to worry, that if a guy hits a home run off him he hits it off me, too, because I called the pitch. I told him he can't expect to pitch a perfect game all the time. He says he knows it but then, when he gives up a few hits, he wants to throw at everybody. It's dangerous for a pitcher like him because his fastball tails in to a right-handed hitter. If he throws at a guy's head and the guy moves his head back six inches the ball will still hit him because it tails that much. He's never seen a guy's career ruined by a beanball, but I have. It's a terrible thing. But he's learning to control himself. He trusts me now, and usually goes along with what I call. Still, he's not afraid to shake me off, which is good, because next year when I won't be catching him he'll have to think for himself. Now when Bruce throws at a batter it isn't to get even, it's because he has an idea. That's what makes him different from most young pitchers. He always has an idea when he's on the mound. He's a lot smarter than most guys in this game. That's why he's always talking about going to college. Maybe that's good and maybe it isn't. I don't know. Maybe he's got too many alternatives and he should concentrate only on baseball or else he won't make it."

"I like Woody," says Bruce Kison. "And I respect him. He knows a lot of baseball and he's helped me a lot. But I still can't understand what he's doing here. When I first came to Waterbury I was shocked at the number of older guys, like Woody, who were just hanging on. They started calling me "Sweetie" and "Punk," and at first I didn't like it, but now I don't mind. I get along good with them, although I never let myself get too close because you never know when you'll have to push one of them for a job. I don't have much to say to their wives either. I feel kind of uncomfortable around them. I mean, what am I supposed to say? I can't understand why they're here. What kind of life is this for a woman, traveling around the country like a gypsy? And the fans! I don't bother with them either. Some of the older guys like Woody go out of their way to be nice to them because they want some friends here if they ever have to come back. I don't plan on ever coming back to Waterbury. . . . Oh, I guess that's not quite true. I might come back for a year if I had to. But I could never make a career of playing in towns like this. Me, a 33-year-

79

old relief pitcher in the minors! I'd have to say no to that. But I have trouble focusing a few months ahead in my life, much less two or three years."

In the top of the seventh inning with the score still tied 0–0, Waterbury loads the bases with two outs. Woody Huyke steps into the batter's box. He chokes up on his thick-handle bat and hunches over the plate. His feet are close together and he holds the bat close to his chest. His practice swings are nothing more than little push strokes emanating from his chest outward. His stance and swing have changed considerably since Hastings, Nebr., 12 years ago. He used to stand spread-legged, with a long, thin-handle bat cocked far back by his shoulder so that it would generate the maximum power when he swung.

Woody works the pitcher to a 3 and 2 count, then fouls off three straight pitches with little half-chops. He is thinking that if only he can wear this pitcher down with enough foul balls he can work him for a walk, which will force in the go-ahead run. But finally the pitcher throws a fifth straight strike and Woody is forced to swing. He hits a high foul ball behind the plate. Without even waiting to see if it will be caught, Woody walks back to the dugout, drops his bat and begins buckling on his shin guards. The ball is gloved by the Elmira catcher to retire the side.

"Man, one of these days I'm gonna kill a cloud," says Woody to the fans. "I don't understand it. I swing just like Ted Williams said. I read his book from cover to cover and he said to swing up, so I swing up. I don't understand it." Woody is smiling now as he finishes clipping on his chest protector and grabs his mask. "Maybe it's because

I'm not Ted Williams. Huh? You think that could be it?" and he walks back to the plate to catch Kison's warm-ups.

In the bottom of the seventh the first Elmira batter lays down a perfect bunt. Woody pounces on the ball and throws out the runner. Then he picks up the bat and hands it to the Elmira bat boy. The second batter grounds out to third base. The third batter works Bruce to a 2 and 2 count before he strikes out on a tailing fastball. Woody rolls the ball out to the mound and comes jogging back to his chair, smiling. "Extra innings, man, we're gonna get them now. I just feel it. You know I can feel it when we're gonna get them. No kidding. I love it. What else could I do that I love so much, you know what I mean? This is a beautiful ball game."

In the top of the eighth of this regularly scheduled seven-inning game, Waterbury scores a run on a walk, a stolen base, an error and a sacrifice fly. In the bottom of the eighth, Bruce Kison retires the side on seven pitches to preserve his fifth victory of the year against four losses. As he walks off the mound he meets Woody Huyke, smiling, at the dugout and they shake hands. Woody says, "Bruce, I had a dream I would catch two shutouts today. No kidding! I dreamt it last night."

The End of Innocence

$\mathbb{B}$ruce Kison, the Pittsburgh Pirates' 6-foot, 5-inch, baby-faced pitcher, is hunched over the steering wheel of his green Volkswagen, his knees jacked up around his ears, his eyes glassy and wide, his pink face pressed close to the windshield and splashed with the greenish lights and shadows shooting past his car. He is traveling through the bowels of the Squirrel Hill Tunnel at over 80 miles per hour in pursuit of a police escort that he has lost but whose sirens are echoing off the walls around him. "I never speeded before," says Kison as he slides Santana's recording of *Black Magic Woman* into his stereo tape deck. The music is barely audible over the strung-out whine of his car's engine and the sirens. Kison begins to sing—"Black magic woman/change your evil ways"—just as his car is about to smash into the rear end of a blue Galaxie. Without missing a note or stabbing the breaks, Kison jerks the steering wheel to the left. There is a shriek, the smell of burning rubber, and the Volkswagen—tottering on two right wheels—shoots into the left lane, simultaneously cutting off a white Cadillac whose driver nails his palm to his horn. Without looking back, Kison ticks his left hand out the window and extends the middle finger from a clenched fist. With his right hand he raises the volume of his stereo until it is full blast. The steering wheel is cradled between his knees. The Cadillac's driver keeps his palm on his horn. Kison, his left hand still showing displeasure, the steering wheel still cradled between his knees, nails *his* palm to *his* horn. He sings louder. "BLACK MAGIC WOMAN/CHANGE YOUR EVIL WAYS." The sirens grow closer, piercing the night. The walls of the tunnel quake, rumble, seem about to fissure, and it all so terrifies drivers up ahead that they swerve into the right lane and stop in order to avoid this possessed little Volkswagen hurtling through the Squirrel Hill Tunnel like some misshapen, misguided missile whose pilot, gone mad, is now, at precisely 8:03 P.M., Sunday, Oct. 17, 1971, thirty-three minutes late for his wedding.

A few hours earlier, Kison, naked except for a towel around his waist, had stood by his stall in the visiting team's locker room of Baltimore's Memorial Stadium and contemplated the chaos about him. The room was packed almost to a standstill with writers, photographers, baseball executives, well-wishers and players all celebrating the Pirates just-completed World Series victory over the Baltimore Orioles. A battery of television cameras stood planted in the center of the room, their cables slung low overhead like black clotheslines. People ducked under them as they moved about the room congratulating one another. The cameras were aimed at a brilliantly lighted platform where Roberto Clemente, Steve Blass and Danny Murtaugh were being interviewed by a sleek, nervous-looking Sandy Koufax. Behind them on the same platform, players jostled for position to be next interviewed. Photographers wandered the room with cameras held high overhead. They poised frequently at the edge of a group of writers and flashed their cameras down at the sweaty, grinning faces being interviewed. The reporters moved from player to player in a pack, pressing their subjects against their lockers and, with furious scribbles, recording for posterity such comments as: "You can't take anything away from the Orioles. They're a helluva team"; "Yes, I certainly do think the best team won"; "This is the greatest buncha guys I've ever been with. The greatest, know what I mean?"

Those players not being interviewed or photographed, particularly those whose contributions to this celebration were negligible, celebrated the most exuberantly. They shrieked and slapped at open palms. They hugged and kissed and tousled one anothers' hair, and, inevitably, when the champagne arrived, they sprayed it at anyone and everyone within range. Standing by his stall, Kison said to a friend, "I told you to wear old clothes in case we won. You'd better put your coat in my locker. They don't care who they spray with that stuff." He shook his head and added, "Boy, it sure seems an awful waste. I'd rather drink it." He took a bottle from a nearby case and offered it first to his friend. While his friend sipped, Kison said, "This has got to be the most exciting day of my life. Imagine!

85

Winning a World Series and getting married on the same day!"

While his teammates celebrated, Kison dressed quickly and slipped out of the room. He followed a police escort through a cheering crowd, across Oriole Avenue, behind a brick high school and into an open field where a police helicopter was waiting to take him and his best man, Bob Moose, to Friendship Airport. At the airport they would be met by Jack Piatt, a friend of Pirate broadcaster Bob Prince and the president of Jetcraft Incorporated, an executive air travel company. Piatt had arranged the loan of his needle-nose Lear Jet to fly himself, Kison, Moose, and his wife Alberta, who was eight months pregnant, directly to Pittsburgh in time for Kison's scheduled 7:30 P.M. wedding to Ann Marie Orlando, a 21-year-old student nurse, at the Churchill Country Club. It was already 6:30 P.M. by the time Bob Moose reached the helicopter. He was weaving unsteadily. His gray baseball uniform was drenched with champagne and his black Pirates' cap with the gold peak was resting on his head at a jaunty Howdy Doody angle.

With much clattering of blades, the helicopter rose slowly and noisily. It hovered about 20 feet off the ground and then began backing away until a man below flapped his arms. The nose of the helicopter dipped sharply, its tail rising and drifting slightly to the right, and then it began moving forward, its whirling blades blowing the tall field grasses flat against the ground until they looked white in the late afternoon sun. Kison stretched out his legs as far as he could in the cramped compartment, and while Bob

Moose sang, he said, "You know, I've never been in one of these things before." The helicopter continued to rise above telephone wires, trees, houses until it was high over a scooped-out Memorial Stadium. It circled the stadium once, twice, each time rising higher, before finally spinning free of the stadium's orbit and moving in a straight line over a cemetery below. Along the way, its plexiglass windows vibrating, the helicopter frequently faded to the left and right on gusts of wind, but still continued to move forward at a faint right angle and with an agonizing but relentless slowness that was carrying it toward a reddish-orange sunset only partly shrouded by a dark cloud.

The flight to Pittsburgh lasted 22 minutes. During that flight Jack Piatt, an immaculately dressed man with graying hair, opened a small bar and poured his party drinks. He offered a toast to Kison's wedding. Then, grinning, he leaned forward and asked Kison what was happening back in the Pirates' locker room.

"Nothing much," said Kison.

For the remainder of the flight Piatt extolled the virtues of his Lear Jet. "It only costs $800,000," he said, as he poured another drink for himself, Kison, Mrs. Moose and her husband, who was falling asleep against her shoulder. "It can climb at 6000 feet per minute and it cruises at 525 miles per hour. There's no sense of flight in one of these babies." Piatt sat back and added, "You ought to get one, Bruce. It's the only way to go." Outside, the plane hung silent and motionless over a field of cloud. The sky above the clouds was a pale, diminishing blue that was bleached almost white as it approached the sun off to the left of the

87

plane. The sun was huge and round and white. It seemed devoid of heat but gave off only shafts of light that hit the tips of the left wing and exploded into a thousand silver slivers that so blinded the plane's occupants they were forced to draw the curtains and darken the cabin.

When the plane landed at 7:14 P.M., Piatt made a certain production of checking his watch. He shook his head emphatically and said, "God Bless Jetcraft!" Kison, unsure of the proper response, thanked Piatt for the use of his jet. Then he, Mrs. Moose and her husband, who was becoming more awake, hired a battered yellow taxicab for the drive to Three Rivers Stadium, where they would pick up their cars and be escorted to the Churchill Country Club. On the way to the stadium they passed an endless stream of cars and pedestrians moving toward the airport to greet the Pirates, who would arrive later. Most of those walking on the side of newly excavated Highway 60 were teen-agers. They carried hand-painted signs and Bucs' pennants. They held hands. They sang. They waved to passersby and generally looked like a peaceful remnant of Woodstock Nation, somehow lost in time and place; they certainly gave no hint of the violence they would later unleash on their city.

As the cab approached the city limits it moved more slowly in the thickening traffic. From the back seat, Bob Moose ordered the driver to "charge right through any red lights! We got an important man here." The driver, sucking a cut finger, looked in his rear-view mirror at the man in the soaked baseball uniform and shook his head. Nor did the driver seem willing to "floor it" as Moose repeatedly suggested. Finally they came to a stretch of open road and the driver pressed his foot more heavily on the accelerator.

"Heh, man! Cut that out!" said Kison from beside him. "We got a woman with child back here! So what if I'm a few minutes late? They can't start without me, can they?" Then he slid down in his seat, folded his hands behind his head and said to no one in particular, "It still hasn't hit me yet. I mean, everything that's happening to me."

In the summer of 1970 Bruce Kison, a native of Pasco, Wash., was struggling along with a sore arm and a 4-4 record with the Waterbury Pirates of the Double A Eastern League when he was inadvertently picked by *Sports Illustrated* as the subject for an article on minor league life. From the moment of his first interview to the end of the season he did not lose another game for Waterbury. The following summer, after being sidelined most of the spring with an infected tendon in his pitching hand, Kison won 10 of 11 starts with the Charleston Charlies of the Triple A International League before he was called to Pittsburgh after the All-Star break. The Bucs, at the time, had been making a shambles of their division. Suddenly their pitching talent, never too thick when healthy, found itself stretched to transparency by an injury to the arm (and not the mouth, as most Buc fans had prayed) of their ace, Dock Ellis. Kison was pressed into service immediately. He won his first two starts, the second a two-hit shutout. He was 4-2 after a month of starts before he ran into a streak of bad luck, during which time he pitched

89

creditably enough but was only registered losses or no decisions. He finished the regular season with a 6–5 record and a 3.41 ERA, amid talk that as a 6-5, 170 pound side-armer he needed more stamina and another pitch before he would become a winner in the majors.

Because of his slight tailspin at the end of the season, Kison did not expect to see much, if any, service during the National League playoffs between the Bucs and the Giants. He watched from the safety of the bullpen as the Bucs won two of the first three games despite less-than-inspired pitching from their aces, Ellis and Steve Blass. When Blass failed to last for a second time in the fourth game, Kison was called in with the score tied at 5 apiece in the third inning. It was obvious to most that manager Danny Murtaugh wanted to save such veteran relievers as Dave Giusti for the crucial later innings, and that he intended Kison as only a stopgap performer who, hopefully, could manage three outs before he would be pinch-hit for in the next inning. But Kison so handily dispatched the heavy-hitting Giants that Murtaugh, sensing a new character was being written into his scenario, did not pinch-hit for him in the fourth inning. Nor did Murtaugh seem particularly upset when his skinny rookie extinguished a Buc threat with a routine ground ball. Murtaugh's flexibility paid off, as Kison meticulously fleshed out his role with one scoreless inning after another.

When Kison finally exited in the seventh in favor of Giusti (a squat, somber-looking man in marked contrast to Kison's stretched-out, pink-faced innocence), he had created for himself a role of almost heroic proportions.

Throwing mostly rising and screwballing fastballs and a
small but quick slider, he had limited the Giants to two
hits and no runs in 4⅔ innings and had received credit
for the Bucs' pennant-clinching victory. What impressed
most people about his performance was that it seemed un-
expectedly cool and professional coming from a rookie
who, uncharacteristically, seemed not the least impressed
either by the circumstances in which he now found himself (besieged by writers) or the batters he had just faced.
(In fact, he had so intimidated 40-year-old Willie Mays,
who ran for shelter whenever one of Kison's fastballs came
swooping in on his aged body, that one sportswriter prayed
openly for his beloved Mays to retire and spare him the
sight of any future humiliations at the hands of such an
upstart.) It was assumed by fans and writers alike that
Kison's apparent coolness both on the mound and in post-
game interviews was really nothing but the naïve facade of
an awestricken youth. This assumption sprang, in part,
from Kison's manner (he is quiet to the point of taciturn-
ity); but mostly from his deceptive appearance. At 21,
Kison looks 15. He has a gawky adolescent's body, all arms
and legs and little torso. His face is long and fine-boned
and dusted with a peachlike fuzz. It is dominated by eyes
so wide and blue as to appear unblinking, stunned, pos-
sessors of a three-dimensional quality distinctive to those
animals, like gazelles, who seem always one twitch from
flight. Yet Kison isn't timid or stunned. Nor does he possess an unfathoming innocence akin to Billy Budd's. He is
simply a direct if slightly unfinished young man, whose
parts are well formed if too few. His directness owes only

91

a small debt to innocence, however, and more to an instinct so blunt as to be at times brutal. He does or says nothing that is superfluous, and, in fact, seems as straight and simple and obvious as the age in which he lives is circuitous and convoluted and unfathomable.

When the World Series began in Baltimore few people expected Kison to play a prominent part in its resolution. His performance in the playoffs was viewed as the aberration of a novice that owed more to luck and propitious circumstances (which in all likelihood would not be repeated this year) than to any talent he might possess. He remained, in the eyes of most people, a baby-faced rookie on whom one could not rely in such a pressurized situation as the Great American Classic. (Oddly enough, Kison was only one year younger than another first-year pitcher, Vida Blue, of whom people expected a great deal more than he delivered in a similar situation.) Heroics in World Series play were the private reserve of such steely-eyed veterans as Dock Ellis, and were certainly not the domain for a youth, who, it seemed, divested himself of his beard each morning with the aid of only a hot towel. Even Kison admitted he did not expect to see much action in the Series. He was even apologetic for the good fortune that had brought him into an event which some of his teammates, like Bob Veale, had had to work eight years to reach. And Veale, a nine-year veteran who had fallen out of favor with the Bucs' management, would probably see as little service as Kison.

Kison enjoyed the anonymity with which he was greeted in Baltimore. It allowed him to eat his meals in peace and then sit unnoticed in the chaotic, baggage-strewn lobby of the Lord Baltimore Hotel and watch the spectacle of his first World Series with a detachment denied his more illustrious mates. Manny Sanguillen, for instance, could not step from an elevator without being besieged by autograph seekers who were drawn to him as much by his perpetual grin as by his blindingly-white Panama suit with its lapels equal to the wingspan of a 747. On the other hand, Dock Ellis, a heavy-lidded, petulant-faced man who seemed always bored or angry or maybe just in need of sleep, was too forboding a presence to be approached for autographs. Besides, he was always striding across the lobby in that high-waisted, stomach-thrusting strut of his to answer one of his innumerable pages ("Call for Mr. Dock Ellis!"); or else he was surrounded by sportswriters to whom he was expounding on the quality of his hotel accommodations, as if he were not only the Bucs' starting pitcher in the first game of the 1971 World Series but also a dark-skinned Temple Fielding in wedge heeled boots.

At night, while Kison sprawled across his bed and watched television or telephoned his fiancée in Pittsburgh, the ballroom of the Lord Baltimore would be noisy with sportswriters and baseball people from all over the country. At dinner one might find himself beside Paul Richards, vice-president of the Braves, his leathery face as mean and inscrutable as a hawk's; Jim Fanning, general manager of the Expos, a trim, impeccably dressed man with a lipless smile; John Mullins, special assistant for the Astros, with whom one insanely expects to begin all conversations with "What's up, Doc?" because he so closely re-

93

sembles a certain cartoon character; Joe Torre, National League batting champion, looking unusually thin but still as dark and sinister as a villain from "Gunsmoke"; Dave Bristol, manager of the Milwaukee Brewers, perpetually smiling, smiling, smiling . . . and available; Dick Young, sportswriter for the New York *Daily News,* a jut-jawed little man who seems always to be arguing with cab drivers and who considers himself the moral conscience of sport; Milton Gross, sportswriter for the New York *Post,* a slightly hunched-over, furtive-looking man who talks only out of one side of his mouth as if distrusting even what *he* has to say; Roger Angell, sportswriter for *New Yorker* magazine, a balding, bespectacled, mustachioed man who seemed to be constantly brushing dust from his slacks, and was once described as a writer of "ethereal" sports pieces; Arthur Daley, Pulitzer-prize winning sportswriter for *The New York Times,* a tall, gray, dignified-looking man with an incongruous Gomer Pyle grin and the dazed look of one who has just caught the drift of a conversation that has long switched to another topic; Walter "Red" Smith, dean of American sportswriters and a recent addition to *The New York Times,* a white-haired, pink-faced little man whose nose is always sniffing heavenward as if in search of a fresh lead or, possibly, just a carrot; Al Hirshberg, author of *Fear Strikes Out,* a diminutized version of J. William Fullbright, who once asked Dick Young to autograph a baseball, after which he told Young, "It's my nonentity ball, only nonentities can sign it."

After dinner the sportswriters adjourn to a makeshift bar

94

in the hallway outside the ballroom. There, over bourbons and scotches, they form small circles and rehash past Series, spin tall tales, swap guesses as to the outcome of this Series (heavily favored toward the Orioles because of their experience and pitching). Or maybe they just test a potential lead on their cohorts, a lead that if favorably received might appear in tomorrow's column. In one circle, Red Smith, rocking on his heels, sniffing heavenward, is speaking in a thick Irish brogue. Arthur Daley, his arms folded tightly across his chest, stands silently beside him, and Dick Young, with anxious eyes, edges ever closer to this prestigious twosome.

In another group, Milton Gross is telling a young sportswriter covering his first World Series that he, Milton Gross, was the first "chipmunk" of sportswriting.

"What's a chipmunk?" says the novice.

Milton, speaking out of the left side of his mouth, explains to the novice that a "chipmunk" is a sportswriter who asks his subject an outrageous question (like Popeye in "The French Connection": "Did you pick your feet in Poughkeepsie?") with the hope that the stunned subject will respond with an unprepared, and equally outrageous, answer.

"But why a 'chipmunk?' " repeats the novice.

"Because in the long run," says Milton, "all we do is nibble around the edges."

"But what about the heart of a story?" says the novice. "Don't you ever try to get to the heart of the matter?"

Milton smiles and shakes his head. "Kid, when you've

been in the game as long as I have you'll learn there is no heart."

Inside the ballroom, after the dishes have been cleared away and only cups of coffee or glasses of scotch and bourbon remain, the general managers, farm directors and managers of various teams huddle at the round tables, one of which is possessed by the Atlanta Braves, another by the New York Mets and still another by the Chicago White Sox. At the latter, Chuck Tanner, smoking a long cigar and looking confident, is whispering to his director of player personnel, Roland Hemmond, who is scribbling on a napkin with a felt-tipped pen. Finished, Hemmond shoves the napkin in his coat pocket and stands up. He nods briefly to Tanner, who sits back in his chair, takes a long drag on his cigar and watches Hemmond scurry over to the table of another American League Club. Hemmond talks animatedly with that club's farm director and a trade is proposed which, if consummated, will alter the destinies of men, like Bruce Kison, who are blissfully unaware that their destinies are, at this precise moment, being decided by others.

"Sometimes I think the Series is just an excuse for the front-office people to get together and make trades," says one such executive. "The only problem is that after enough scotches who the hell knows whom he traded to whom? I have this horrible dread of waking up with a hangover some morning to answer a telephone call from another GM who just wanted to confirm the fact that last night, at about midnight, I traded my entire infield to him for a shortstop who is batting .231 in the Carolina League. B-r-r-r-r."

When the ballplaying began, the heavily favored Orioles took the first game handily. They knocked Dock Ellis out of the game in the third inning and, as it developed, out of the Series, too. After the game a weary Murtaugh told reporters that Ellis had pitched with a sore arm. "You gentlemen didn't see the real Dock Ellis out there today," he said in a barely audible voice, and then added that Ellis was through for the Series. Beside his locker, Ellis, surrounded by reporters for the last time this year, was saying, "There wouldn't have been no World Series without my factin'. I gave you guys something to write about before it even began."

Sunday's second game was rained out, but on Monday the Birds picked up where they left off, grabbing a 1–0 lead in the second inning and adding two more runs in the fourth before Murtaugh relieved starter Bob Johnson with his skinny rookie Bruce Kison. Appearing in his first World Series, Kison threw nine pitches. Eight of them were balls, and he was promptly yanked in favor of his future best man, Bob Moose. The Birds erupted for six more runs in the following inning, and for the rest of the game the record 53,239 fans in Memorial Stadium yawned. The crowd was stirred only briefly in the seventh inning when Linda Warehime, the female member of the Birds' ground crew, came streaking up the left-field line to dust off the bases, as is her custom.

A few years ago Linda was barely a teen-ager. With her

long-legged, boyish stride, her floppy white bellbottoms and her long yellow hair flying in her wake, she looked like anyone's tomboy neighbor streaking across the field. When she reached the infield she would dust off each base with her broom and also dust off the shoes of her beloved Orioles—Boog and Davey and Mark and Brooks. When she worked her way around to the opposing team's third-base coach she would either dust off his shoes, too, plant a demure kiss on his cheek, or else play a harmless prank on him, any of which would draw a roar of approval from the partisan crowd.

Now, well into her teens, Linda Warehime came onto the field in the seventh inning of the second game wearing white, thigh-high boots, black satin hot pants and a snug-fitting orange jersey. Her once-boyish stride had shortened considerably. It had also taken on a certain attractive twitch which, combined with her new outfit, lent her an air decidedly not tomboyish. When she reached the Pirates' third-base coach Frank Oceak she lowered her broom as if to dust off his shoes, then swept dirt all over them. Oceak, the 59-year-old father of two daughters, aimed a swift kick at Linda's backside, but fortunately for both, he missed. Later, Oceak admitted that he really did want to kick Linda Warehime because, as he put it, his team was losing and it was no time to be making sport of such a serious affair. Besides, Oceak added, "there's a time and place for everything."

In the locker room after the game, which the Birds won 11–3, Kison was asked by sportswriters if he had been nervous in his first World Series appearance, and if that hadn't accounted for his wildness.

"No," he said. "I just wasn't used to the mound, and that might have thrown my control off. But, no, I wasn't nervous."

When asked if Murtaugh would use him again in the Series, Kison replied, "I don't think about those things. I just sit back and wait and let things fall into place. If he uses me, okay. If he doesn't, okay, too. I just hope we win, that's all." (The following day Kison picked up a paper and read that his wildness was caused by his nervousness at being in his first World Series, which was to be expected of such a rookie.)

The third game moved both teams to Pittsburgh (a town described by one writer as "full of shot-and-a-beer guys whose sole ambition is to own a house off the highway with a propane gas tank in the backyard") and its massive concrete and felt billiard table known as Three Rivers Stadium. This is one of those perfectly proportioned ovals similar to ancient coliseums, but so oppressively modern as to be without odor (except, when new, of fresh gypsum); without blemish (no worn patches of grass, no obstructive pillars, no garrishly advertisement-plastered outfield fences); and without character (one can buy a private, glass-enclosed, sound-proof booth so removed from the action that its occupants can be seen watching the game on portable television sets). Its rows of brightly painted seats bank gradually away from the playing field like seats in a movie theater. This eliminates obstructed views but also places most seats beyond the first few rows at a great distance from the field. At such a distance on a muggy after-noon the players become blurs of gray and white, gliding in slow motion over a perfect pale-green cloth, pursuing a baseball that can be heard but not seen, performing an eerie ballet akin to that of the tennis players in the movie "Blow-Up."

In the third game the baseball was also unseen by the Oriole batters. They managed only three hits off the serves of veteran Steve Blass, and the Bucs won their first game of the Series 5–1. Blass, a 29-year-old veteran of modest success, is known amongst sportswriters as the Bucs' resident intellectual and wit. He is also a pitcher of only ade-quate talent but great desire, and he throws the ball with such a flurry of arms and legs that he resembles a young boy trying to impress his elders and willing to fall on his face, if necessary, to do it.

Still, the Pirate victory was looked upon by most knowl-edgeable fans as simply a delaying action, a prolonging of the Orioles' inevitable triumph. The win was brought about by that superior individual effort (from Blass) one must expect in such a confrontation of professionals, but which, in no way, had a bearing on the accepted script.

Now, in the fourth game, events and characters would revert to type. This was the first night game ever played in a World Series and, broadcast on television at prime time, it would draw 100,000,000 viewers, not to mention the paltry 51,378 fans who would watch at the stadium. Be-fore the historic game, Ken Smith, curator of the Baseball Hall of Fame in Cooperstown, N.Y., scrambled all over the field collecting mementos of this occasion—such as the first baseball ever used in a night World Series game, which, in fact, it wasn't, since it was plucked spotless from a box and handed to Smith.

Standing around behind home plate during batting practice was Bowie Kuhn, the commissioner of all baseball. Kuhn, a husky, dignified-looking man in a gray pinstripe suit and black wingtip shoes, was led to a spot behind home plate by a group of photographers. He was given a monstrous metal cup, which is the World Series Trophy, and told to stand in that spot until he was joined by Earl Weaver and Danny Murtaugh. When the two managers appeared on either side of Kuhn, one of the photographers yelled, "Okay, smile Commissioner," and when he did, the photographers began taking pictures. While the commissioner grunted and tried to smile under the immense weight of the trophy, Murtaugh and Weaver chatted across him and his trophy, as if the trophy, one empty vessel, was suspended by another. When the photographers had taken enough pictures they unceremoniously left the commissioner for greener pastures. Weaver trotted back to his dugout and Murtaugh, his hands stuffed in his back pockets, walked deliberately back to his. The commissioner, still smiling and sweating, stood by himself with his trophy for a long moment before finally saying, "For chrissakes, somebody help me with this thing or I'll be here all night."

The photographers, meanwhile, had spotted Linda Warehime in the stands alongside the Orioles' dugout. Linda had become something of a minor celebrity since Oceak's misdirected swipe at her rump. She was standing in the midst of a group of teen-agers clamoring for players' autographs. Linda would have been indistinguishable from that group if not for the sullen, abused look on her pouty face, which indicated she was not used to the neglect she was now experiencing in a foreign stadium. She brightened considerably, however, when the photographers spotted her and led her onto the playing field. When they began taking her picture in front of the Orioles' dugout, the other teen-agers realized with a groan that they had had a celebrity in their midst without knowing it.

The game commenced according to script. The Orioles scored three runs in the top of the first before Pirate starter Luke Walker, a taciturn Texan who dresses solely in black, was spared further embarrassment. When his replacement, Bruce Kison, stepped from the golf cart (built in the shape of a black and gold baseball cap) that had brought him in from the bullpen, there was a barely audible groan from the Pittsburgh fans. It was as if the appearance of this elongated, pink-faced rookie was a sign of Murtaugh's resignation to the inevitable Baltimore triumph. Nor did the fact that Kison retired the side with one pitch abate this feeling of despair. However, when the Bucs scored two runs of their own in the bottom of the first, their fans, expecting a speedy replacement for Kison, took heart. When he took the mound in the second inning they hoped Murtaugh was just waiting to pinch-hit for him in the next inning. They would forgive Kison any future transgressions if he could just manage these three outs before retiring. Kison, working quickly but unhurriedly, with that sweeping right-to-left sidearmed delivery

of his, retired the first two batters he faced. Then Paul
Blair hit a pop fly that bounced in front of Roberto Clemente and sprang on the tartan surface over his head for
a double. Kison, undaunted, retired the next batter on an
infield fly.

Murtaugh did not pinch-hit for Kison in the second
inning; nor in the fourth (by which time the score stood
3-all); nor in the sixth. During those innings, in full view
of the largest audience ever to watch a baseball game,
Bruce Kison pitched flawless baseball. In this flawless performance one must include, not exclude, the three batters
he hit with his pitches, which set a World Series record.
Those Orioles, bruised in spirit as well as body, were simply being served notice by Kison that despite his virginal
appearance he was not a person with whom one could take
liberties. In fact, Kison has always hit a high proportion
of batsmen throughout his three-year professional career.
(He once hit eight batters in a single game, which his team
won.) His difficulty stems from a fastball that breaks
sharply in on a right-handed batter at the last second. This
break is often misjudged or overlooked by most batters
and results in bruised ribs. Also, because his curveball is
such a brief affair, and anxious batters tend to lean far
over the plate in anticipation of pasting it off the right-
field wall, Kison must protect himself by firing an occasional pitch a bit inside. This combination of a batter
leaning one way and a fastball breaking the other accounts
for his frequently plunked batsmen. There is a feeling
among Kison's close friends that he is not particularly upset by these accidents, and that he feels such occurrences

more than compensate for his limited repertoire (two basic pitches) and his virginal looks. Yet, in the fourth game of the Series, he claimed that the three hit batters were results of his youthful wildness (strangely enough, he did not walk a single man during that span).

By game's end Kison had put himself into baseball's record books in another way. He had become the first pitcher to win a night World Series game. He did it by allowing the Orioles only Blair's bloop double and no runs in 6⅓ innings, before retiring in favor of Giusti, who preserved the 4–3 victory. Four days later when the Bucs defeated the Orioles in the seventh game, Earl Weaver would say in a televised interview that the fourth game was the turning point of the Series, and that Kison had been the pivotal figure in the Bucs' reversal. Weaver explained that with a three-run lead in the first inning, and with a rookie pitcher at their disposal, the Birds should have waltzed off with that game, giving them a 3-1 edge and, eventually, the Series. "It was Kison who turned the whole thing around," said Weaver. "Without that nutty kid we would have won it."

The moment Kison entered the Pirates' locker room after the fourth game, writers, photographers and television cameramen, who had been occupied with his teammates, came running toward him from all parts of the room. He was surrounded and immobilized before he could reach his locker. Flashbulbs exploded in his face. People shouted orders and questions at him. A television cameraman, his camera slung over his shoulder like a bazooka, yelled at Kison to look his way, and when he did the cameraman flashed a bright light in his eyes. Kison raised a hand to shade his eyes, and as he did, a television commentator stuck a microphone under his nose and began asking him questions. The sportswriters were forced into silence as they waited their turn at Kison. They grumbled and fidgeted until the cameraman extinguished his lights, and then they simultaneously attacked Kison with a dozen questions. For just a split second a look flickered in Kison's eyes like that of a terrified animal about to flee, and just as quickly it was gone, replaced by a look devoid of all expression. Kison folded his arms across his chest and then, towering gazellelike above the writers yapping at his heels, he began to answer their questions.

"Were you as nervous today as you were in the second game?" asked a writer.

"I don't know," said Kison. "I had trouble getting the ball over the plate in the second game so they said I was nervous. If I'd have gotten it over they would have said I was calm. So I guess you can say I was nervous in the second game but I was calm today."

"What's your telephone number?" asked another writer.

"I don't know."

"You don't know your own telephone number?"

"I never had to call myself before."

"Do you mean to tell us you weren't nervous in that second game?"

"Everybody brings in nerves, nerves, nerves," said Kison. "I don't think about being nervous. I just tried to do better this game than last, that's all."

"If the Series goes seven games," said another writer, "do you think you'll be able to make your wedding?"

"When I set the wedding date I had been told by some of my teammates that the Series would be over before then. I was told it never went into the second week of October. I should have looked into it myself. That was my mistake. But if I'm in Baltimore Sunday then that's where I'm supposed to be. I'm here to help win the Series first and then get married afterwards."

"Bruce," said Milton Gross, "now that you're famous, do people recognize you when you walk the streets?"

"I don't walk the streets."

"Is your fiancée good-looking?" asked another writer.

"She's okay."

"I mean, is she a really good-looking girl, you know?"

"What do you think? Boy, that was a stupid one."

"What do you think of major league sportswriters?"

"They're all right. They haven't stuck a knife in me, yet."

While Kison was talking, Milton Gross, who was directly under his nose, began arguing with a radio interviewer over rights to the next question. The argument grew louder and louder until Kison broke off in mid-sentence and rolled his eyes heavenward. Finally the argument abated, and Kison was asked if his childhood dreams have come true.

"Yes, my dreams have come true, and then some."

For a third time a writer asked him about his wedding.

"Why is everyone making such a big deal about the wedding?" Kison said. "It's no big deal. If I can't make it back to Pittsburgh Sunday we'll have to change it, that's all."

While Kison was talking, Bing Crosby, part-owner of the Pirates, walked by him and said with a grin, "Well, they know where Pasco is now, Bruce." A few of the writers broke away to interview Crosby, who Kison kept referring to as "the Bo-bo-bo-bo-man."

"How often do you shave?" asked a writer.

"Every day," replied Kison.

"Do you need to?"

"I wouldn't shave if I didn't." Suddenly there was a commotion by the telephone on the wall. One of the Pirates' trainers motioned for Bruce to answer the phone. While Kison talked, the writers edged closer to eavesdrop. One of them said, "Who is he talking to, the President?" Someone else said, "He's talking to President Nixon," but they were not sure until Kison hung up and returned.

"Who were you talking to, Bruce?"

"That was my father and mother and some friends of the family, and, oh, yes, my dog."

"What'd they say?"

"Nothing much. My mother and father and the friends congratulated me. The dog didn't say anything. He can't talk."

From the outer edge of the group the writer who asked Bruce about his fiancée's looks said to another writer, "It's hard to tell if he's a bright kid or not. I thought he'd say his fiancée was sensational, a knock-out, something I could use. But he doesn't say what you'd expect. I don't know. Maybe he just isn't too bright."

107

"How do you show pressure inside?" asked a writer.

"I don't know," said Kison. "You tell me."

"Don't you feel *anything* inside?"

"I guess."

Another writer told Kison that Frank Robinson, from whom he elicited snarls and stares when he plunked him in the ribs, was still furious with Kison for his performance. The writer asked Kison to comment on Robby's anger.

"I think you're just trying to cause friction there," said Kison. "I don't want to answer that question."

From behind the mass of writers, Steve Blass, yesterday's hero, could be heard saying, "Yeh, my wife will probably want to sleep with Kison tonight. Last night was my night. She's a real front-runner, you know." The writer he was talking to laughed, and he was soon joined by other writers who began interviewing Blass. A clean-cut, strong-jawed man, Blass not always had such an easy time with writers. A few years ago he found an old World War I German helmet and he took to wearing it in the locker room, to the delight of his teammates. When Dick Young discovered his antics he wrote a blistering column attacking Blass for making a mockery of something against which millions of American boys died fighting.

"I couldn't see how anyone could take that so seriously," says Blass today. "But still I got rid of the helmet. I even decided I should hate Dick Young forever. But no matter how hard I tried I couldn't. The best I could do was stay mad for what I considered an honorable period of time. Now we get along fine."

108

Today Blass gets along fine with most sportswriters who find in his self-deprecating humor (despite its predictability) the perfect tonic for tired stories. In fact, at 29, Blass is so in tune with the thinking of sportswriters that often he senses precisely what they are seeking and supplies it so smoothly and effortlessly as to make it seem spontaneous. He is also a master at sidestepping delicate queries with affable grace. It is a quality, says freelance writer Melvin Durslag, that all ballplayers must acquire if they are to survive. "They build up a tolerance to some questions and automatic responses to others," says Durslag. "Bruce Kison hasn't cultivated this yet, but he will, and maybe that's a shame. Right now, Bruce refuses to answer dumb questions in a clever way, but is willing to answer good questions in a fresh new way. But soon he'll answer them all with safe clichés."

Blass agrees. "Bruce will have to learn how to handle writers eventually," he says. "Sometimes he makes judgments too soon without considering all the possibilities. I've tried to tell him he can't be too quick in evaluating people, especially writers. But Bruce is flexible. He'll learn as he gets older. He'll become more aware, which is a shame really. It's like a loss of innocence. He won't be this Bruce Kison anymore. He'll be a new Bruce Kison, because people demand more from us than we're really capable of giving."

It is midnight when Bruce Kison finally emerges from a shower into an all-but-deserted locker room. Dripping, he moves to his stall and begins drying himself. He is incredibly long and bony. His ribs show, and yet he claims

109

he has already begun to put on weight since he's arrived in the major leagues. "I've gained ten pounds," he says. One wonders where.

"Jeez, I hated all this attention," he says to a friend. "I must have acted like a real fool in front of those writers. Did I? Jeez, I hope not. Aw, shit, I know I did. A real fool." He throws his towel into the center of the room and begins dressing and muttering to himself. Bob Veale, the only other player in the room, comes over to Kison and says, with mock solemnity, holding an imaginary microphone in front of Kison, "Tell me, Kison, how's it feel to set a World Series record by hitting eight batters in three innings?" Kison smiles and says nothing. Veale adds, "And to be such a big hit with all those sportswriters, too? My goodness, Kison, tell me, how's it feel?"

When Veale is gone Kison says of him, "He told me to go into the locker room between innings so my arm wouldn't stiffen up. He's always helping me out like that. Jeez, sometimes I feel sorry for him. I wonder why I'm so lucky. I see him sitting alone at his locker, not saying anything, and I wonder what he's thinking. He has to watch me get all this attention in my first year and he's been here eight years."

On the morning after his fourth-game triumph, Kison arrived at Three Rivers Stadium at nine for a television interview with Sandy Koufax. He was smoking a cigar, which made one feel his father ought to be told.

Kison and Koufax stood halfway down the third-base line and chatted while the television cameramen set up their equipment in the visitor's dugout. A brilliant sun hung over the center-field bleachers and had already begun to cut through the morning mist. It was directly at Kison's back, making him visible only as a dark silhouette, while Koufax, to Kison's left, was minutely visible in every detail. Koufax, at 35, looked as sleek and jittery as a greyhound. He wore a navy blazer with an NBC television crest on the breast pocket. He also wore a red shirt and a red and navy patterned tie; gray double-knit slacks; and black alligator-skin loafers with a brass buckle on the tongue. As Koufax chatted with Kison, his microphone hanging at his side, he constantly tugged at his shirt collar, stretched his neck, smoothed his already smooth hair and glanced at the cameramen. Kison stood spread-legged and motionless. His hands were stuffed into his back pockets. His shirt hung outside his pants and he wore cowboy boots. When the cameraman signaled Koufax to begin, he raised the microphone to his lips, assumed a smile and began asking Kison questions. Kison replied in a monotonous voice. His hands remained in his back pockets and his eyes drifted over Koufax's head to the deserted stadium around him. The first three takes were unsuccessful, and with each new take Koufax became increasingly annoyed. Finally, when Koufax blew a fourth take, the cameraman signaled for him to continue. Koufax yanked the microphone away from his mouth and said, "Goddamn it, no we won't! Bruce doesn't want to live with that, do you Bruce? And I sure as hell am not gonna make a fool of myself in front of millions of viewers."

The fifth take began with Kison saying, "I was very

displeased with my performance in Baltimore in the second game. . . ."

On the morning of the seventh game of the World Series, Bruce Kison sat at a table in the coffee shop of the Hilton Hotel in Baltimore and waited impatiently for his scrambled eggs. He had returned to Baltimore with his teammates after the fifth game, which the Bucs had won 4–0. Nelson Briles, a travel-weary veteran, who does an excellent imitation of Humphrey Bogart, had pitched a superb two-hitter in that game. Afterward in the Bucs' locker room he was almost in tears as he told sportswriters, "This has to be the biggest thrill of my career."

The Orioles had staved off a possible four-game sweep by the Bucs with a 3–2 victory in 10 innings of the sixth game to set the stage for today's deciding contest. The importance of the contest, in which he would be the first reliever in case Blass faltered, and the uncertainty about reaching his own wedding that night in Pittsburgh, made Kison unusually irritable. His irritation had also grown from what he considered to be undue attention heaped upon him by sportswriters and photographers ever since his fourth-game triumph. He did not like his instant notoriety, he said.

To pass the time while he waited for his breakfast, Kison tried to objectively reevaluate his pitching of the past year so as to best be able to negotiate his 1972 contract with the Pirates' front office. He decided that his 10 victories in Triple A, his six victories during the regular season with Pittsburgh and his two playoff and Series victories qualified him as an 18-game winner. Furthermore, his victory in the playoffs and the one in the Series would be worth about a half-million dollars to the Pirates, and, possibly, if they won today, a million dollars. He deserved a small portion of that cash, he said, and he wondered just how much he should ask for. (Ironically, when the Bucs divided up their World Series and playoff booty, they failed to give Bruce Kison a full share.)

"It's funny," said Kison, "but I don't care that much about money. I mean, here I am talking about all this money, and if I had to I'd play for nothing back in Pasco. I wouldn't play every day for nothing, but still I'd play. Money doesn't mean that much to me yet. I'm not a clotheshound like some guys on the club. Clothes are just something to wear, necessities, like food. I don't love to eat. I eat until I'm content, that's all. But it seems the more you taste big-league life the more you want—or think you want. You get caught up in things that never meant much to you before. You become something different. I'm not the same person I was a year ago, six months ago or even a few weeks ago. When I was a kid I admired the milkman. I wanted to grow up and be just like him. Then you grow up and your sights change. Your goals get larger than they were, and Pasco is no longer enough for you. I still love to go back to Pasco and hunt, but I don't think I could go back and drink beer on Saturday nights for the rest of my life.

"I once said I could never stay in baseball unless I was in the major leagues; that if I didn't make it I'd go back to college and get my degree. College is getting farther and farther away from me. I can see myself as an organization man in the minors now. I wouldn't like it much, but still I can see myself doing it.

"It doesn't take long in baseball before you become like everyone else. I mean, when you first come to the majors you hear guys talking about things, like girls and stuff, and you think, that isn't me. I'll never be like that. But pretty soon you realize you'll evolve into what everybody else is sooner or later. But I don't think I'll mind that. It doesn't look so bad now. And when it happens, all I'll think about is protecting myself up here. I know that right now there's some kid in the weeds, some kid riding a bus someplace, and he's checking my ERA in *The Sporting News* just like I did at Waterbury. That's funny when you think of it, isn't it?"

Bruce Kison looked around for his waitress. "Jeez, where is she? I only ordered eggs." He sighed disgustedly and then continued. "I guess I've learned a lot up here. I learned that baseball is for the owners and sportswriters and fans, not the players. We just perform for them. For instance, the other night a guy came to my hotel room and asked if he could come in and talk to me. He said he was a great Pirate fan and that he followed me closely and thought I was great. So what could I say? Anyway, he kept talking and talking about how great I was and how no one will believe it when he tells them he was in Bruce Kison's room, and all the while he's looking at me with these big eyes like I'm some kind of hero or something. Finally I said to him, 'It isn't that big a deal, you know.' He just looked at me and said, 'It is to me.' Then he left.

114

"People idolize us too much. They give us importance we don't deserve. I know I may be the first pitcher ever to win a night World Series game, but I don't feel that important. I still think of myself as a kid. But maybe that's just me. Baseball is still a sport to me. It's a business to everyone else. I'm just a piece of property, I know that. But that doesn't mean I want people to make a living off me all the time. Take my wedding, for instance. I don't want people to make a living off my wedding. That's a helluva way to start out."

Suddenly the waitress appeared with his eggs. She placed the platter of eggs in front of Kison and he looked at them for a second. He picked up his fork, picked at the eggs and then said, "I wanted them well done. These eggs aren't well done." The waitress picked up the platter and returned to the kitchen.

Kison laughed a little. "That's funny. I'd probably never have done that a year ago. But there are also a lot of things I used to do, I'd never do now. When everybody's looking at you, you can't always express exactly what you feel. I think that's the most important thing I learned up here. I mean, you don't tell everything you know anymore."

A Talent for Refusing Greatness

A small boy is trying to bounce a bat off the rubber floor of the Cleveland Indians' dugout and catch it as it bounces back. He misses repeatedly. Out on the field the Indians are taking batting practice while the Oakland A's play pepper in front of their dugout.

"Heh, Moon," calls Alvin Dark, the Cleveland manager, from behind the batting cage. "Weren't you supposed to pitch today?"

Oakland pitcher Johnny "Blue Moon" Odum looks up from his pepper game and says, "Supposed to, Alvin. But I wasn't feelin' too good today." He grimaces and massages his right shoulder.

"Jeez, that's too bad, Moon," says the Cleveland manager with an evil little grin. "Sudden will be very disappointed. You know, I saved Sudden just for you today."

"I appreciate that," says Odum, "but I guess I'd rather pitch tomorrow."

117

"But we ain't playing tomorrow," says Dark.

"I still rather pitch tomorrow," says Odum, and players on both clubs break into laughter.

"Sudden" is the nickname of the Cleveland Indians' 27-year-old left-handed pitcher, Sam McDowell. McDowell was given that name by opposing batters, who when asked to describe how his fastball approached the plate, invariably replied, "All of a sudden, man, all of a sudden." Ever since, McDowell has been signing autographs, shirts, photographs, gloves, baseballs and just about anything but checks, "Sudden" Sam.

On May 6, 1970, Sudden Sam McDowell fired his sudden pitch past 15 Chicago White Sox batters in eight innings. He lost the game 2–1. When Blue Moon Odum heard of McDowell's feat he shook his head in disbelief. "Man, if I had Sudden's stuff I'd win 25 games every year."

Some people thought Odum had complimented McDowell—until they checked McDowell's six-year major league record and discovered he had never come close to winning 25 games. In fact, McDowell had barely won that many games in two years. With what has been called by most major league hitters "the best stuff in baseball," McDowell has managed records like 17-11, 13-15 and 15-14. His best year was in 1969 when he finished 18-14. His career record is 89-80, although admittedly he has never played with a good team. But then again, neither did Robin Roberts when he was winning 20 games all those years for the Phillies—and Roberts never had "the best stuff in baseball."

Odum was not the first man to be critical of McDowell's

lack of ability to win baseball games, although it appeared to be the first time McDowell was stung by such a remark. He responded by winning his next seven of eight decisions for a 10-4 record, a 2.40 ERA and 146 strikeouts in 146⅓ innings. At one point he had all the club's eight complete games to his credit. By July most opposing pitchers were discovering mysterious sore arms that disappeared the day after they missed their turns against McDowell. (Odum's was not mysterious, however, and he was eventually placed on the A's disabled list.)

To casual observers it would seem that Sudden Sam had finally silenced his critics. But this was not the first time McDowell reeled off a flurry of victories, silenced his critics and then stumbled into warm mediocrity by September. In 1966 he was 4-0 in the first month of play, and then, after a brief sore arm, managed only a 9-8 record despite a 2.88 ERA and 225 strikeouts in 194 innings.

It has been said that Sudden Sam McDowell possesses a talent even greater than his assorted pitches: the talent to refuse his greatness. Like a character from an Ayn Rand novel, he has discovered he has the kind of awesome talent that stills all motion in its wake—only Sam McDowell does not know why all motion is stilled in his wake, and furthermore, he could not care less. He seems to be afraid that if he let his talent grow to its fulfillment he might cease to possess it, and it, in turn, would possess him. So he treats his talent like some unruly growth he must periodically prune before it becomes unmanageable.

When Sudden Sam McDowell emerges, hunched-over, from the darkened runway into the sun-drenched Cleveland dugout, he looks like some monstrous pin-striped Polar bear emerging from a winter's hibernation. He stands 6 feet, 6 inches tall, weighs 235 pounds, has a natural snarl to his lips and throws a fastball with such force that his catcher, Ray Fosse, worries that someday he will lose all circulation in his catching hand. Today, McDowell also has a heavy, sandy stubble growing over his large, square jaw.

"I never shave on days I'm gonna pitch," he says, in a deep, understated growl. "I try to look extra mean on those days. It helps me get batters out." He also does not talk to writers or fans, sign autographs or pose for pictures on those days.

When McDowell sees the young boy bouncing the bat off the dugout floor he walks up behind him, reaches over his head and grabs the bat. The boy whirls around, looking up and up and up in terror into that unshaven, shadowed face.

"Watch this," says McDowell. He bounces the bat handle on the floor, catches it as it springs back, flips it over his shoulder, lets it slide down his back, pulls it through his legs, bounces it one more time and then executes a perfect pirouette before catching the bat on the rebound.

"Wow, Sudden, how'd ya ever learn that?"

"Easy," says Sudden, the corners of his eyes crinkling slightly. "I practice every time I hit a home run."

"Will ya teach me?"

"I can't right now," says Sudden, and he navigates three dugout steps in one leap. "I have to go practice 'The

World's Greatest Drag Bunt.' " McDowell claims he is the second best hitter on the Cleveland club (Vada Pinson is the best, he admits), so he sees no sense in practicing his hitting when he could be spending his time more valuably by practicing his drag bunt.

"The only thing I get satisfaction from," he says, "is accomplishing something I'm not supposed to be able to do. I live for challenges, and once I overcome them I have to go on to something new."

But Sam McDowell is *not* the second best hitter on the Cleveland Indians, and he knows it. However, he is so talented—or rather blessed with talent—that he probably could be if he ever put his mind to it. But the possibility of achieving a goal and actually achieving it are one and the same thing to McDowell. That is, to prove one *could* be the greatest hitter is the same as *being* the greatest hitter in Sudden's estimation. Therefore, why bother to prove it? This is precisely why McDowell never has a won-lost record commensurate with his ability. He knows he's proven time and time again that he has the best stuff in baseball (he holds just about every American League strikeout record and, along with Sandy Koufax, is the only pitcher ever to average over one strikeout per inning), therefore he feels he is naturally the best pitcher in baseball. Right? Wrong. Wrong to most people maybe, but not to Sudden Sam McDowell. Like many extremely talented people, Sam McDowell does not judge his accomplishments by conventional standards. His challenges, and their eventual resolution, are very private affairs inde-

121

pendent of either the approval or disapproval of anyone else.

As McDowell walks to the warm-up mound in the right-field corner, fans come running from all parts of Municipal Stadium to watch him throw. He does not warm up like most pitchers, soft-tossing 40 feet from their catcher as if trying to prolong the inevitable trek back to 60 feet, 6 inches, where their deficiencies become glaringly apparent. McDowell begins throwing 80 feet from his catcher, and almost from his first pitch the ball is swallowed in the catcher's mitt with a thunderous crack. And when Sudden throws his first curveball he does not cautiously spin it up to the plate in a lazy arc, "just to get the spin right." Instead, he fires it with such force and snap that it collapses at the plate like a mallard shot on the wing. By the time Sudden finally works down to 60 feet, 6 inches, it sounds as if there is a small thunderstorm in the Cleveland bullpen.

It is obvious that McDowell takes great delight in watching his pitches behave even when he's only warming up. And he admits to often concentrating so much on his individual pitches and their perfection that he loses sight of everything else. His individual pitches then become his goal rather than simply the means of attaining some larger goal—a victory, for instance.

"I try to break things down to their simplest element," he says, "and sometimes I guess I do it to an extreme. For instance, a game to me is just a series of individual challenges—Me against Reggie Jackson or Me against Don

Mincher. If I find I can get a guy out with a fastball it takes all the challenge away, so next time I throw him all curveballs. If I don't have a challenge I create one. It makes the game interesting."

Against Oakland this night, McDowell breezes along with a shutout until the fifth inning. In the fifth he walks the A's seventh batter, hangs a change-up to the eighth batter for a single, then tosses a half-speed fastball to pitcher Pat Dobson, who lines it to left field to score two runs. After another single and a walk load the bases, Sudden strikes out Sal Bando on three fastballs, then fans Reggie Jackson on fastballs thrown so hard that rookie Steve Dunning says in the dugout, "My God, I didn't see them. Not one of them."

"No, I wouldn't say Sudden is the toughest pitcher I ever faced," says Reggie Jackson. "Now, don't get me wrong. I like Sudden and I think he's got the greatest fastball, curveball, slider and change-up of any pitcher I ever saw. I call him 'Instant Heat.' But still, I don't mind facing him. That's not because I hit him so easy, either, because I don't. It's just that Sudden simplifies things out there. He makes it like it used to be when we were kids. You know he's gonna challenge you, his strength against yours, and either you beat him or he beats you. And if you do beat him with a home run or something, hell, it don't bother him that much. He's not greedy. He lets you have a little, too. And he won't throw at you, either, because he's too nice a guy. He knows that with his fastball he could kill you if he ever hit you. You see, baseball's still a game to Sudden, the way it should be to all of us. Hell, I'd pay to see him pitch because I know he enjoys himself so much. Do you know he's got 12 different moves to first base? That's a fact! When he was going for his 1500th strikeout he was trying so hard he fell down on a pitch to me. I took it for a third strike. I loved that, though. That's why I look forward to facing him even if I don't hit him a helluva lot. But someday I will. Me and Sudden will be around for a long time, and one of these days I'm gonna connect with one of his sudden pitches and watch out! But still, I have to say that Sam McDowell isn't the toughest pitcher I ever faced. As a matter of fact, I think he'd be tougher if he had less ability. Sounds crazy, huh? But it's true. Sudden's just got too much stuff."

Alvin Dark agrees that it is possible for a pitcher to have too much stuff. But Dark refuses to admit that is true of his ace left-hander. As a matter of fact, Dark refuses to admit much of anything about Sam McDowell, treating all such questions with the same dread little girls treat the offer of candy from strange old men.

"Some guys, you break them down pitch by pitch," says Dark, "and they should be 20-game winners. But when you add them all together again the best they do is 15 or 18 wins. Something's missing. I don't know what. Just something. Now, I'm not saying that's the case with Sudden. I'm just saying that's the way it is with some guys."

Most members of the Cleveland Press corps and the Tribe's front office would not be so ambiguous as Dark. They definitely think there is something missing from

McDowell that has prevented him from achieving the greatness they predicted of him for the past six years.

When McDowell was first brought up from the minors in 1964, he was a scrawny 21-year-old rookie with a blazing fastball, a $75,000 bonus and a reputation for eccentricity. The fans, the press and the front office immediately billed him as "the new Bob Feller" and waited, impatiently, for Sudden Sam to fulfill his potential. He didn't. He either failed or refused to fulfill the role everyone else had defined for him, both as a pitcher and a personality. Instead of winning pennants, as the Tribe did with Feller, they finished sixth, fifth, fifth, eighth, third and sixth, respectively, in the six years McDowell's been in the majors. And in none of those years has McDowell been any better than just a decent pitcher.

At first it was hard for people to understand how a pitcher with McDowell's stuff could never be as good as the sum of his parts. But when it became apparent that this was the case, they reacted with bitterness. This culminated in the remarks of a local radio personality who said that Sam McDowell would never be anything more than a second-rate pitcher because "he had a million-dollar arm and a ten-cent head."

Although most people did not agree with the tone of that remark, they did agree with its substance. How else could you describe a guy with the best stuff in baseball, who thinks he has to have a beard to get batters out?

Once people resigned themselves to the fact that Sam would never equal his potential, life was easier for everyone involved. The fans grew to love him (they voted him

"Man of the Decade" recently); the writers no longer badgered him; the front office treated him like some mischievous child they tolerated with the forlorn hope that someday—maybe someday—Sudden Sam might "straighten out." Today, it is understood by everyone in Cleveland that Sam McDowell is just a big, likable kid, more talented than most but a big kid nevertheless, who finds it impossible to take anything in life too seriously.

Sam McDowell is standing in his underwear in front of his locker, dressing in his uniform. Tacked to either side of his locker are postcards of bikini-clad maidens. They are healthy, nubile young things modestly enough looking away from McDowell as he dresses. Directly on top of his locker is a small, white figurine of a homely old washer-woman. She is smiling and pointing a finger at Sudden Sam. Written on the base of the figure are the words: "Guess who I like?"

"Hoot, did I ever tell you the one about the kamikaze pilot?" Sudden says. Hoot Evers, the Tribe's coach, looks up from his newspaper.

"No, Sudden, you never did," says Evers.

"Well, this one kamikaze pilot was the ace of the squad," says Sam.

"How come?" asks Evers.

" 'Cause he made 12 successful missions."

"Oh, I see," says Evers, and goes back to reading his paper.

"Sudden, Jeez, did you see this in the paper?" Dean Chance comes over to McDowell and hands him a newspaper, which he begins to read as Chance talks.

126

"What the hell am I gonna do?" says Chance in mock panic. "My financial adviser, Denny McLain, is $400,000 in debt."

Sam finishes the paper and hands it back to Chance. "Why don't you call him and ask him the odds on tonight's game?" says Sudden very seriously.

"Maybe I will," says Chance with a grin, "maybe I will." And he walks into the trainer's room.

"Call him collect," adds McDowell. "Tell Denny I said he wouldn't mind."

When McDowell finishes dressing and is about to go out to the dugout, Cy Buynak, the Tribe's stubby little clubhouse man, comes over and asks why Sam didn't fill out his telephone number on a form Cy needs. Sam tells him he doesn't know his telephone number.

"What do you mean you don't know your telephone number," says Cy, hands on hips, indignant. "How could you not know your own telephone number?"

"I just don't know it," says Sam, sheepishly.

"That's impossible. Everybody knows their telephone number. How you gonna call your wife in case of an emergency?"

"I never thought of that," says Sam. Cy slaps his forehead and walks away muttering to himself. There is a thin smile on Sudden's lips, and it isn't until much later that he tells Cy that he's just moved into a new house and his phone hasn't been installed yet.

"When I first interviewed Sam one day in spring training," says Bob Fitzgerald of WJW-TV, "he told me that Birdie Tebbets, the manager, wasn't pitching him because he didn't like him. I figured I had a scoop until Tebbets told me the reason he wasn't pitching Sam was because he had a sore arm. After that I never knew how to take Sam. Then, just recently, I met his father. He had that same devilish twinkle in his eye that Sam has, and finally it dawned on me that all these years Sam's been putting us on."

At various times in his career Sam has told interviewers that strikeouts mean nothing to him and his biggest thrill was his 1500th strikeout; he never loses his temper and he once threw a ball out of Baltimore Stadium over an umpire's call; records mean nothing to him and he's broken all of Feller's strikeout records; he takes pitching a baseball too easily and he worries too much about pitching; he could never throw at a batter and he would throw at his mother if she hit a home run off him; and baseball means everything to him and baseball means nothing to him.

"I like to give everybody what they want," says Sudden Sam, with a grin. "I used to worry about what the writers wrote until I realized they wrote they wanted to no matter what I said. So I decided I'd make it easier for them by saying whatever they wanted."

Fitzgerald doesn't think that's the only reason McDowell is so ready with a quip or a contradiction. "I think Sam was hurt by the bad publicity he got early in his career. He decided to hide behind all these contradictory statements so that no one would be able to discover who he was and hurt him again. He's just a big kid who's afraid of being hurt, that's all."

As further proof that Sudden Sam is just a big kid in the

128

disguise of a talented giant, Fitzgerald cites his numerous hobbies. In his spare time Sudden manages to collect and build guns, put model boats together in bottles, train German Shepherds, shoot pocket billiards and paint still-lifes. At first glance these interests may seem haphazard, but they do have two things in common. Each can be worked at in solitude; and Sam views each and every one as a personal challenge, isolated from the approval of anyone but himself. For instance, although he admits he is a good enough pool shooter to become professional, Sam refuses to play for money. As one of the few registered gunsmiths in the country, Sam could make a small fortune plying that trade, but instead, he builds and restores guns for his own satisfaction. "I don't sell them, but if I ever did you could hunt all day with them and hang them up as showpieces when you got through. That's how I make them." As a painter of still-lifes, Sam has one small problem. "I try to make the thing I'm painting more perfect than it is. So frequently people don't recognize what my painting is supposed to represent."

Sam began training German Shepherds when he bought a Starin German Shepherd to protect his wife and children. "The Starin is the largest of all the German Shepherd breeds," he says. "They're supposed to be only one-master dogs and I couldn't resist training mine so he would obey my wife and kids. Now he'll obey any kid in the neighborhood. When we have a party for the kids we just put the Starin outside and he scares off all the adults. I never trained him to obey adults," he adds, with a grin. "Just the kids."

Besides his hobbies, Sam also owns a pizza parlor and a pool hall in Monroeville, Pa., a small, exclusive suburb of Pittsburgh. And he is a salesman for "Holiday Magic, the Organic Cosmetics."

When Sam goes on road trips with his team, he carries so much baggage (adding machines, paints, easels, gunsmith tools, etc.) that he has to live alone. "There wouldn't be room for anyone else with all that stuff," he says. "I always bring my stuff because I don't like to go out of the hotel when we're on the road. For instance, New York scares me to death, so I just eat downstairs in the hotel, then go back to my room to fool with my hobbies or watch television."

Many people are bothered by Sam's numerous hobbies, because he treats them with the same interest he does his baseball. It annoys them that he refuses to treat his pitching ability with any more reverence than his ability to build guns or shoot pool.

"He ought to be ashamed of himself," says a big-league pitching coach. "Hell, if I had his talent I'd win 20 games every year."

The reason Sam takes as much interest in his hobbies as in his pitching is that he views life as nothing more than a series of isolated challenges, none of which is any more important than the others. Baseball is a part of his life, just as guns and pool are. But few people achieve greatness until they are able to divorce themselves from everything except their profession.

"To be a great pitcher or anything," says Herb Score, "you have to give up a lot. Some guys just don't want to make the sacrifice. They'd rather do great now and then, than be great."

Writers and managers are particularly annoyed with Sam's refusal to devote his life entirely to baseball. The writers try to pressure him into greatness through bitter articles, while the managers try different tactics.

"When I caught Sam a few years ago," says Duke Simms, now a catcher with the Dodgers, "Joe Adcock decided to call all of Sam's pitches from the bench. In Anaheim one night Sam had super stuff but Adcock kept getting him in trouble. Finally Adcock loaded the bases in the sixth inning and I turned to the dugout for the sign, but he turned his back on me. He made Sam get out of it on his own. I think Sam eventually lost that game. But managers have always tried to make Sam throw the pitches they wanted, and he's seldom had success at it."

"Managers are mostly ex-hitters," says McDowell, "and they seldom have any respect for pitchers. They don't understand that all pitchers are unique and have to be handled differently. Most managers think pitchers are dumb because we like to do our own thing. Yet we couldn't be too dumb because every year they're changing the rules to make life easier for the hitters.

"I never wanted to be a baseball player. I'd just as easily have been a teacher or any other 9-to-5 job. There's no certainty to baseball. I'd like the certainty of a 9-to-5 job. But my father saw I had the talent so he forced me into it. I never thought I was that good anyway. When I signed, all the clubs were promising to send me right to the majors. I was so terrified of that I signed with the Indians

131

because they promised to send me as low as possible, to Class D ball. Even when I made the majors I never thought I was that good. The other players were always gods to me until a few years ago. I used to start every game with the hope I just wouldn't embarrass myself out there. I've always felt I was forced into the majors before I'd harnessed my mental and physical abilities. Even now, no matter how great people say I am, I'll never believe it. . . . What's bothered me most about people all these years is how much they've demanded from me. No matter what I do they want more. It's never enough. They seem to be envious of my talent, although I never thought I was so gifted."

To Fly Like the Gulls

I don't ever think about it," he says. "Philosophically, that is. Why do I do it? What does it all mean? That doesn't interest me. I only know it excites me. It's the one thing I do in my life that excites me." Tom Seaver, untanned, wearing a gray t-shirt and baggy Bermuda shorts, is standing in the sand of Madeira Beach, Fla., only a few feet from the Gulf of Mexico. He is holding a piece of string to which is attached a kite that is only a speck far off in a cloudless sky. The sky overhead is aswarm with the flap and caw of sea gulls. Big, grayish, heavy-breasted birds, they must beat their wings furiously, stomachs heaving, necks straining forward, so that for one brief moment they can level off and glide with a hard-earned and uncommon grace.

"Aren't they fascinating!" says Seaver. "The way they work at it! I could watch them for hours. I'd love to fly like the gulls, but I can't. So I pitch. If I couldn't pitch I'd do something else. It wouldn't bother me much. But if

I *could* pitch and I wasn't, that would bother me. That would bother me a lot. Pitching is what makes me happy. I've devoted my life to it. I live my life around the five days between starts. It determines what I eat, when I go to bed, what I do when I'm awake. It determines how I spend my life when not pitching. If it means I have to come to Florida and can't get tanned because I might get a burn that would keep me from throwing for a few days, then I never go shirtless in the sun. If it means when I get up in the morning I have to read the box scores to see who got two hits off Bill Singer last night, instead of reading a novel, then I do it. It makes me happy to do it. If it means I have to remind myself to pet dogs with my left hand or throw logs on the fire with my left hand, then I do that, too. If it means in the winter I eat cottage cheese instead of chocolate chip cookies in order to keep my weight down, then I eat cottage cheese. I might want those cookies, but I won't ever eat them. That might bother some people but it doesn't bother me. I enjoy that cottage cheese. I enjoy it more than I would those cookies because I know it'll help me do what makes me happy.

"Life isn't very heavy for me. I've made up my mind what I want to do and I do it. I'm happy when I pitch well, so I only do those things that help me be happy. I wouldn't be able to dedicate myself like this for money or glory, although they are certainly considerations. I know, also, if I pitch well for 15 years I'll be able to give my family security. That's a realization. But it isn't what motivates me. What motivates some pitchers is to be known as the fastest who ever lived. Some want to have the greatest season ever. All I want is to do the best I possibly can day after day, year after year. Pitching is the whole thing for me. I want to prove I'm the best ever."

Tom Seaver is the youngest pitcher in the history of professional baseball to sign a contract for over $100,000 a year. He has averaged 19 victories per year from the first moment he began pitching for a team, the New York Mets, whose normal finish during his tenure has been fifth place. At the age of 27 and after five years in the majors, he has won 95 ball games. Walter (The Big Train) Johnson, who won more games than any modern pitcher, won 80 games in his first five seasons in the majors. Before celebrating their twenty-seventh birthdays, Grover Cleveland Alexander, second to Johnson, won 70 games; Sandy Koufax, 68 games; Warren Spahn, 44 games; and Bob Gibson only 19 games.

George Thomas Seaver has one of those smooth, boyish, middle-American faces that would be a burden to some men. It possesses that handsomeness so prized in the 1950s of Pat Boone and Tab Hunter, which tempts one to describe it as having too little character, when one would more rightly mean too few characteristics. It is a face of undistinguished parts subordinate only to a single, clear impression of uncluttered good looks.

Seaver stands 6 feet, 1½ inches tall and weighs 210 pounds from November to February, when he indulges himself with an occasional breakfast of fried eggs and beer; he weighs 200 pounds from March to October, when he allows himself no indulgences. He has a squarish, heavy-

135

chested body that tends to fat but is deceptively muscled. His arms, shoulders, chest and thighs are thick with muscles acquired from years of lifting weights. He believes, contrary to the opinion of most pitchers and coaches, that a selective program of weight lifting will add speed to a pitcher's fastball. As proof, he points to himself. As a high school senior in Fresno, Calif., he stood 5-9 and weighed 160 pounds. He was the third hardest thrower on his team, and he did not pick up speed until he began lifting weights in college and had grown to 6 feet and 190 pounds. Because he worked so diligently in developing those parts of his body that relate to his talent, Seaver is highly critical—one might almost say contemptuous—of less conscientious players. He will say of a teammate whose chest is noticeably undeveloped, "Do you know he hit 20 balls to the warning track last year? Twenty! Another 10 feet and they would have been home runs. I know I'd find the strength to hit those balls another 10 feet."

Although not conscious of it, Seaver cannot hide his disdain for men who he feels have not fulfilled their potential. For Seaver, a man's talent is not just a part of the man. It is the whole man, or at the very least a mirror of the whole man. To treat one's talent carelessly is indicative of a weakness in character that he cannot abide. He once said of a former pitcher who was reputed to have dissipated a promising career, "What a fool he must be to throw it all away like that! If you don't think baseball is a big deal, don't do it. But if you do it, do it right." Seaver studiously avoids such men, as if their weakness was a contagious disease. He prefers to pass his free time with men like Bud Harrelson and Jerry Grote, who have made the fullest use of their talents, no matter how ordinary.

Despite Seaver's weight lifting, there are certain parts of his physique that are noticeably undeveloped. His waist, for instance, is thick with soft flesh. It is a constant source of kidding for his wife, Nancy, who will say, "He has an old man's waist. Really, he does! He is a lot like an old man, you know." This kidding does not bother her husband in the least since he knows a tightly-muscled waist will add nothing to his talent, and as with most things that do not add to his talent, he has only a passing interest in them. (The perfect way to chill a relationship with Seaver, however, is to make a slighting remark about his talent. No matter how much in jest that remark might be, he will grow silent as a stone while the jester's laugh dies in his throat.)

Seaver is not a vain man. He could no more lift weights in front of a mirror to build an Adonis physique than he could tell an obscene joke in public. He seems to have no real desire to call attention to himself, and if he is at all conscious of the image he presents in public it is only up to but not beyond the point when it offends his own sense of propriety. He dresses neatly but indistinguishably in the clothes he receives from Sears Roebuck and Co., to whom he is committed in business. The only real attention he seeks is when he is on a pitcher's mound, and even then one senses that he does not demand it for himself but for his superb and unquestioned talent.

"After I won 25 games in 1969," he says, "I became engulfed in a lot of publicity and recognition. It was like

137

being caught up in a cloud. People who never met me were making judgments about me, and things were happening to me I had no control over. Then I had this fabulous realization—at least it was fabulous for me—that I had to cut all this stuff out of my life. I had to come back to myself, to what was most important to me, to be the best pitcher I could. Now I don't care about publicity. I don't worry about what people say or write about me. I can relax and be what I am. And what I am is basically a dull guy. No one interviews me much anymore. Even my success is kinda dull. At least, it looks dull to everyone outside myself. But to me it's fascinating!

"I used to think you could reach a point where success would become a bore. A boredom with sameness. But now I know that just as I'm refining my pitching, I'm refining the pleasure I get from it. A victory used to give me pleasure, and then a well-pitched inning. Now I get great satisfaction from just one or two pitches a game. I get in a situation where I have to apply everything I know, mentally and physically, on just one pitch. It all comes down to this pitch. I have to think what I should do and then make my body do it. That's a beautiful point to reach for an athlete. A light goes on in your head and you realize that everything you've done in your life has been for this moment. Things you've been building for years, things you never knew you were building, are right there for you to use. Suddenly, you're the most confident person in the world. There's no doubt in your mind what you can do. You sense you can achieve perfection for just this moment. That's a great thrill for me. It's not a jubilant type of thrill, but a great satisfaction that comes from knowing that for one specific moment I can achieve perfection in something I've devoted my life to."

At 27 years old, Tom Seaver has reached this point in his development as an athlete (a point few men ever reach) because as a youth he was blessed with only modest size and ability. He says of himself then, "I was small and I didn't throw very hard. In my senior year of high school I won five games and lost four. Jeez, but I'd never been the star of any team! Even at USC I had to work hard just to be a starter. Pitching has always been awful hard work for me. I never had anything handed to me. I was aware of my physical limitations at 14. I had to adjust. It was a burden then, but obviously it's helped me."

Pitching became for Seaver, at 14, not only a physical activity but a mental one. He was forced by the limits of his talent to become conscious of all those aspects of his craft which, although secondary to sheer ability, were at least within his power to cultivate. He discovered, for instance, that hitters fed off pitchers' mistakes. Then he would make no mistakes. If he could not throw his fastball past hitters, he could at least throw it where they could not hit is solidly. If he could not strike out hitters, he could at least refuse to walk them. "Walking hitters bothered me even then," he says. "It was so free!"

Seaver discovered that the control and quality of his pitches was directly related to his pitching motion. He became conscious of that motion, not as a stylized routine that could hide his deficiencies and assuage the demands of his ego but as something that could be cultivated,

139

created even, in a way that would afford him the maximum use of his modest talents. He learned also to listen when anyone talked about his craft. And if those comments made no sense to him, he still retained them for a moment in the future when hopefully they would make sense and he could use them. (He met Walt Payne, an ex-semipro baseball player, only once. On that occasion Payne told Seaver it would be wise to use his left hand more often than his right so as to avoid injury to his pitching hand. "It made sense right then," says Seaver, "and now whenever I use my right hand for something I'm very conscious of it.")

Seaver also learned how it felt to be shelled unmercifully in one inning and then have to walk out to the mound to begin the next. "It's a terrible feeling," he says. "You want to quit. You feel it's all so hopeless. You have to force yourself to forget the last inning and start all over as if it never happened. Some guys can't do that. They're always fighting things beyond their control."

Such experiences helped Seaver develop an outlook in his youth (or possibly he just discovered what was all along a part of his nature) that has now become the cornerstone of his pitching philosophy. And, if Tom Seaver could ever admit to having something so grandiose, it has also become his "philosophy of life."

"I learned," Seaver says today, "to let my talent dictate what I was on a given day. I learned to adjust to it, its limits, to what it told me about myself. I couldn't do more than I was physically or mentally capable of. If I tried to throw harder than I could, the ball went slower

140

than it normally would. I couldn't fabricate conclusions in my mind about how to pitch to a batter if my mind wasn't ready for them. I couldn't force things. Sometimes in a game I'll concentrate so hard on my motion, trying to get it right, that I have nothing left for the batter. Then I let Grote call my pitches. I just respond physically. I surrender that mental load to Grote and it's one less load I have to worry about. When I get my motion organized I'll take that load back. But if I tried to perfect everything at once, I'd end up perfecting none of them."

For Seaver, more became less. The result was unpleasant. And so he learned to deal solely within the framework of his limitations, to circumvent those limits, to co-opt them. He learned that success lay not in making war against one's limitations but in making peace with them.

The qualities Seaver developed in his youth are precisely those any athlete must have if he is to excel. However, the pattern through which he acquired them was the reverse of that which most athletes follow. The first discovery a young athlete often makes is that he possesses an uncultivated talent—the ability to hit, run, throw, etc.—that allows him to glide with little effort or thought to a point where that talent alone is no longer enough. Faced with fading success, he must begin cultivating the peripheral adjuncts to sheer ability—control, discipline, expertise—that his early explosion of raw talent made unnecessary, but without which that talent will now never be fulfilled.

Sandy Koufax is a perfect example of such an athlete. He reached the major leagues on the strength of his extraordinary left arm, and then struggled for seven years to develop those qualities (primarily control and expertise) that his arm had earlier made unnecessary. Only when he developed them at the age of 26 did he fulfill his raw talent and become a great pitcher. Because of the absence of such a talent, Tom Seaver was forced to develop at 14 the same qualities Koufax developed at 26. However, those qualities alone made Seaver only a decent pitcher. When he graduated from high school he received no professional offers, and so he enlisted in the Marine Corps. When he left the Corps and enrolled at USC two years later, he had grown and his fastball had matured accordingly. The Dodgers offered him a modest $3000 bonus but he declined in favor of USC, where his development continued. He began a program of lifting small weights on the advice of a friend, Jerry Marz, who told him the added strength would help prevent sore arms and also give his fastball more speed. "I knew a lot of baseball people felt weight lifting hurt pitchers," says Seaver, "but it seemed to help me then and it still does, so I did it."

In one year Seaver's fastball suddenly became explosive. Often, when USC's baseball team scrimmaged the Los Angeles Dodgers, Seaver found himself pitching successfully against major league hitters when only two years before he had had difficulty retiring high school hitters. Major league teams were now besieging him with offers of up to $50,000 for his signature. He eventually signed with the Milwaukee Braves, who shortly thereafter lost him to the New York Mets because of a signing irregularity. "At the time," says Seaver, "I was 21 years old and I didn't understand the magnitude of what had happened to me."

What had happened was that Seaver's physical talent had finally gained pace with all those less tangible qualities he had been cultivating in his youth, and he had become as complete a pitcher as was possible for a man his age. He possessed superior speed, stamina, control, expertise and self-discipline, and unlike most young pitchers he would not have to spend valuable time developing them. In fact, he possessed them to such a degree that within one year of his signing he would win 16 games for the tenth place Mets; be voted to the National League All-Star team (to which he's been selected every year he's been in the majors); become the National League's Rookie of the Year; and three years later earn the Cy Young Award as the best pitcher in the National League; and be generally acclaimed by baseball professionals as the greatest pitcher in the game today and quite possibly who ever lived.

"I appreciate my talent more than most," says Seaver. "I appreciate the things it's brought me. I had to put a lot of hard work into it. Some guys never know the gift they have." And because his talent is more conscious creation than gift, because it is his by acquisition not inheritance, Seaver possesses it, rather than is possessed by it, as few athletes ever do. He has a greater understanding of what it is, its limits and strengths; of how he acquired it; of how he should retain it; and, most importantly, of how he should continue to refine it. And so, perhaps more than any athlete who ever lived, it is within his power to determine the level of greatness his talent will achieve.

On April 21, 1972, Tom Seaver defeated the Chicago Cubs 2–0 for his second scoreless victory in as many starts in a season that was barely a week old. His opponent was Burt Hooten, the rookie who had pitched a no-hit, no-run game only five days before. Against Seaver, Hooten was just short of brilliant. In seven innings he allowed the Mets three hits and struck out nine with his baffling knuckleball-curve. He issued five bases-on-balls, one of which was intentional. Hooten's performance was worthy of high praise, for it had come on the heels of his no-hitter, with its attendant pressures for any 21-year-old rookie, and had come against Tom Seaver, the best pitcher in baseball. His performance could best be described as that superior effort which, when produced against Seaver, is sufficient to reward its producer with internal satisfaction and a graceful loss. Seaver had been better. He did not walk a man in nine innings. Seaver allowed the Cubs four singles and struck out nine. His performance, which did not stop short of brilliance, received less attention than did Hooten's, however, since it is of the kind one expects from him these days. But it was even more astonishing than Hooten's since it had come shortly after Gil Hodges' death; after a prolonged strike during which Seaver was preoccupied as his team's player representative; after a series of postponed games (due to bad weather) that had supposedly curtailed his throwing; and after an unpleasant spring training during which Seaver experienced the first sore arm of his career. Yet Seaver's mid-season performance so early in a disruptive season was easily comprehensible to those who knew of the meticulousness with which he had prepared for it.

Two nights before, he had been scheduled to pitch

against the Expos in Montreal. The game was rained out, and he was rescheduled to pitch against Hooton and the Cubs on the twenty-first. When the Mets returned to New York the night of April 19, most of the players went directly home from LaGuardia Airport. Seaver, however, got a ride on the team bus to Shea Stadium, which was deserted and in darkness. He went directly to the locker room, put on his uniform, filled a bucket with baseballs and began the long walk across the diamond to the right-field bullpen. He moved with a graceless, plodding plowman's walk, his weight falling on his heels and his head listing to his right as if, with each ensuing step, it might collapse upon his shoulder. When Seaver reached the bullpen he stepped onto the warmup mound and began throwing baseball after baseball against the screen behind the plate. His throwing was illuminated only by the lights from the parking lot. He warmed up quickly but carefully in the mild night air. He was accompanied only by the sounds of his own exertion, and of baseballs plunking against the screen and dropping softly to the ground.

He threw with great effort. His speed and curve and control came slowly, and only after much grunting and cursing in the darkness. He threw with a tightly constricted motion that seemed small compared to the loose, spread-out deliveries of pitchers like Gibson and Koufax. Constricted, yet thoroughly planned, for Seaver has worked diligently to cut away "all the excess crap my motion does not need." He has excised no vital parts, so his motion is a perfect compromise between flamboyance and deficiency. If it is not so esthetically pleasing as it could be; if it does

145

not approach the grace of those gulls, still, it is mechanically perfect. And it is perfection, not grace, that Seaver seeks, since he long ago decided that alone was within his grasp. It is a powerful motion, and there is a point in it when Seaver seems to pause for the barest second before exploding toward the plate. He turns sideways, his left leg raised waist-high and bent, his glove and ball hand cupped close to his chest, his shoulders hunched about his ears. He seems to be withdrawing into himself, to be at that single moment in time and place where he and his talent come as close as they ever can to merging into one. He describes this pause as "that point when I pull myself together, mentally and physically, to put everything I have into the pitch."

He needs that moment of intense concentration because —let it be stated once again—neither his delivery nor his pitches are a gift. They do not lie there, polished gems, waiting only to be dusted off for use. They are rough stones that must be painstakingly recut and repolished with every use. And since his success lies not in the overwhelming brilliance of any one gem (he does not have the greatest fastball, the greatest curve ball, the greatest control), but in the proper balance of a host of lesser ones, the recutting must be flawless. The slightest imperfection in one stone destroys the delicate balance of them all in a way that it never would to a more gifted pitcher.

To be a great pitcher, Seaver must be flawless in a way Sandy Koufax never had to be, and it was in the pursuit of perfection that Seaver felt he had to labor that April night in the dark Met bullpen. He threw until he reached the same level of effort and concentration he would have needed against the Expos in Montreal. He continued at this pace for a while and then went home. It was almost 10 P.M. When asked why he put himself through such an inconvenience, he said, "It was my day to throw. I always throw on my day to throw." Two days later, supplied with precisely the edge he both needed and had created, he beat Burt Hooton.

Because of such dedication to detail, it is conceivable that the only thing that could prevent Seaver from reaching the goal he has determined for himself is an event beyond his control—such as the arm injury he experienced this past spring in St. Petersburg, Fla. It was a particularly frustrating injury for Seaver for two reasons: It was the first sore arm of his career, and he could point to nothing as its cause. He had proceeded with his fifth spring training at the same pace he had proceeded with his previous four. "You have to control yourself during the first weeks," he said, "so as not to get hurt." When he felt the first sharp pain in his right shoulder, he was more than a little confused. For the first time in his life he was unable to do what he had devoted his life to. He spent long hours at Miller–Huggins Field in the batting cage along the right-field line, taking out his frustrations on the mechanical pitching machine known as Iron Mike. As Mike wound up to deliver a ball, Seaver would talk to himself, setting up hypothetical game situations such as "man on third—one out—fly ball scores him." Mike delivers. Seaver swings. "Aaaaggghhh!" Pop fly. "God, if I could do that every time!" Mike winds up again. "Man on third—two outs—single scores him." Mike delivers. Slash! Ground ball. "Damn it! Damn it! Damn it!"

When not in the cage or running wind-sprints or fielding bunts, Seaver often approached the Mets' team physician, Dr. Peter LaMotte. He would raise his right arm over his head, dig the fingers of his left hand into that point where his arm and shoulder and back met, and say in a high-pitched, almost whining voice, "What *is* that?" The doctor, a relaxed man who always looks as though he had just returned from the links, would begin a lengthy and clinical explanation of the bruised muscles. Seaver's face would immediately cloud with that exasperated look it so often has when he has no interest in the turn of a conversation. He would listen a few seconds and then interrupt. "But I want . . . I want it to feel . . ." and his voice would trail off in frustration.

After a few days the shock of his injury wore off and Seaver's voice lost its panicky tone. It became curt and passionless as he forced himself to approach the injury as he did all things relating to his talent—as an experience to be understood and absorbed for future use. His questions to the doctor became less pleas and more interrogations. "Which muscles are bruised? How did they get bruised? Will it get worse if I throw?" And finally, when it had healed and he had once again taken his place on the mound to pitch batting practice, he would be able to say: "I don't know many parts of my arm, but I know these. The muscles are called the teres major. They healed only with rest. They were bruised because I began throwing too hard too soon. I hadn't taken into consideration that I'm getting older. I can't proceed during the spring at the same pace I did at 23, I have to expect my body to break down a little with each year. After all, I've pitched almost 1400 innings in five years. I can't go on forever without a sore arm. I just have to be more careful in the future."

Seaver was able to master the experience of his sore arm rather than have it overwhelm him because he has a quick reporter's mind sensitive to experience. This sensitivity to experience and ability to learn from what it tells him about himself has made him the pitcher he is today. Like reporters, however, he is bound to experience. He seems disinclined to intuit without facts, without details, which is why he first had to experience a sore arm before he could adjust to its lesson. It is also why he seems so ill at ease with abstractions, which he describes as not attuned to "the real world I live in." ("Innocence!" he laughs. "Whoever thinks about it? You either have it or you don't.")

Because this sensitivity has proved so valuable in perfecting his talent, Seaver is quite frugal with it. It is not to be wasted on meaningless abstractions. Instead, he is careful to bring it to bear only on experiences "in the real world," and only on those experiences he has decided are of the first importance—*i.e.*, the perfecting of his talent. ("I'm a very introspective guy," he says. "I spent all winter trying to discover what happened to me at the end of 1970 when I finished so poorly. I decided I couldn't pitch with only three days' rest. That discovery made me feel like the genius of the month.")

Seaver is less introspective about those experiences not

relating to his talent. It is not that he places no value on them, but that he feels they exist complete within themselves, and to analyze them would only be a waste of energy that could quite possibly kill the pleasure he gets from them. Such experiences as watching the gulls, ("Aren't they fascinating!") are to be savored primarily as diversions that help fill the void between his bouts with his talent.

"I don't have the stamina and mental concentration to live my life with the same intensity I do baseball," says Tom Seaver. "I'm not a perfectionist in everything. For instance, a few years ago I built a wine cellar in the basement of my home. I used small fireplace flues as holders for the bottles. I laid out 20 flues in each row and 20 rows in all. It was repetitious work but I never got bored. Every flue I laid out was a victory, every row was a 20-game season. The entire 20 rows was a career of 20-game seasons. I loved it. When I finished I began to panel the room. I'd paneled most of it when I came to a water pipe that stuck out of the wall. I couldn't focus on how to panel around that pipe. It was beyond my ability to comprehend. I got bored with it. I almost lost interest. Eventually, though, I did panel it all, but the wine cellar is still far from perfect. But I can live with its imperfections. Some guys couldn't. They have to find out about themselves before they get on that train to New York in the morning. They're always digging deeper than things are. They dig so deep they forget to enjoy life. I enjoy my life. I don't live it at the same pace I do baseball. I can do nothing all day and

150

think it's fabulous. I really could watch those gulls for hours, or just play dominoes with my wife, or watch my daughter Sarah play with her toys. In the winter I like to get up in the morning and sit by a fire. Sometimes I read the paper and sometimes I do nothing but sit by the fire. What do I think about? Ha, I think about how fabulous it is to watch wood burn. Life really isn't very heavy for me. I don't have to pull every weed out of my garden. I don't have to win every three-man basketball game at the YMCA. I can lose as long as I play well. But still, I have to play basketball. Even at the risk of an injury to my arm, I have to play. That's what I am. An athlete. In basketball I don't have to win every game. Maybe I deliberately don't tap this competitiveness in me. Maybe I'm saving it for baseball. It must be like an energy source that has its limits. If I use it up on too many things I'll have nothing left for baseball. Maybe I deliberately leave a few weeds in the garden." He laughs, then says, "I really don't know, though. I never think about such things."

An Angel of His Time

$\mathbf{M}$y career?" he says with a shrug. "It was no big thing. I could never get the knack of what they wanted of me." He takes a delicate sip from a tall glass, purses his lips slightly, then continues. "Oh, I might have had a career if they could have tied me to the mast. You know, like Ulysses? When he heard the mermaids' wailing he wanted to crash against the rocks." He raises his glass to his ear and shakes it gently until the ice cubes tinkle. "You know, Babe—like vodka on the rocks." He smiles. His eyebrows are raised and his mouth is pulled back and down into his jaw. It is a self-mocking smile. It distrusts itself. It is the smile of a man who is accustomed to looking at himself from outside of himself, who takes what he sees with such slight regard that he can smile not at his pun, which is almost cruelly close to the mark, but at the man who can make such a pun.

There is a photograph of Robert "Bo" Belinsky in the May 6, 1962, edition of *The Sporting News*. A slick-looking young man in a California Angels' baseball uniform is surrounded by a number of aging baseball dignitaries and Angels' executives. The older men are dressed in business suits. They are smiling stiffly at the camera while Belinsky, his head cocked slightly to the left, one eyebrow raised, is smiling that slightly ironic, distrustful smile of his at the baseball he is holding up for view. With that baseball he has just recorded his fourth straight major league victory and history's first no-hit, no-run game by a rookie left-handed pitcher. That no-hitter will make Belinsky, at the age of 25, the most celebrated athletic personality in the country. He will be courted by such Hollywood beauties as Ann-Margaret and Mamie Van Doren, and he will eventually marry a *Playboy* Playmate of the Year. He will become an intimate of Hugh Hefner, Walter Winchell, Frank Sinatra and J. Edgar Hoover. He will say to the press, "J. Edgar! Man, he's a swinger! He let me shoot tommy guns at FBI headquarters. I told him if I ever quit this game I might need a job. He said, 'Bo, there'll always be a place for you on the force.' "

Belinsky will also become the star in a prospective television series about a motorcycle loner named Buddy Solo, and in a Las Vegas nightclub act with Mamie Van Doren. Of her "Bo," Mamie will say, "I've got better curves than Bo, but he's got a heckuva better voice. I know, because he sings to me in his car."

Belinsky will be dogged and quoted voluminously by sportswriters, who recognized in him a unique and colorful personality who could always be counted on for such outrageous quips as: "If I'd known I was gonna pitch a

154

no-hitter today I would have gotten a haircut"; or, "My only regret in life is that I can't sit in the stands and watch me pitch"; or, "My philosophy of life? That's easy: If music be the food of love, by all means let the band play on."

In short, within days after his no-hitter Robert "Bo" Belinsky, a former pool hustler from Trenton, N.J., would be heralded as sport's most original and engaging playboy-athlete. His name would become synonymous with a life-style that was cool and slick and dazzling, epitomizing not only the life-styles of such later athletes as Joe Namath, Ken Harrelson and Derek Sanderson, but also those of an entire, ephemeral decade—the Sixties. And eventually, only a few short years later, that same name would become synonymous with dissipated talent.

Bo Belinsky won only 24 major league baseball games in the nine years following that rookie no-hitter. He lost 51 times. He was traded away by five major league clubs and fined, suspended and banished to the minors regularly for what had come to be viewed as his unstable and child-ish behavior. Those same sportswriters who had written adoringly of the rakish Belinsky as a winner became less than adoring with Belinsky the loser.

"There is a race to Bo Belinsky's pad every morning," wrote one sportswriter. "It is a race to see who arrives there first, Belinsky or his milkman. Belinsky has yet to win." Another wrote, "The Angels are about to market a new Bo Belinsky doll. You wind it up and it plays all night, all morning, and three innings in the afternoon."

One morning Bo Belinsky was picked up by the police

155

at five o'clock for throwing a female companion out of his moving "lipstick-red" Cadillac on Sunset Strip. The Angels' fined him, and the girl sued him. On another morning at three o'clock Belinsky was accused of punching a sportswriter in his hotel room. For that incident he was suspended from the Angels and, without a hearing by the commissioner of baseball, immediately banished to the minor leagues. On still another morning, this time at four o'clock, the hotel in which Belinsky and his teammates were staying burned down. While his teammates assembled sleepily in the streets, the manager began to count heads. "My god!" screamed the manager. "He's not here! He must be inside." From behind the crowd a voice mumbled, "Who's inside?" The players and their manager turned around to confront Robert "Bo" Belinsky stepping from a cab, as he put it, "reeking of bitch and booze." The following morning Belinsky explained his fine to the press thusly: "Boys, you know you're going good when you beat a bed check and then your hotel burns down." His record at the time was 1 and 5.

One night Belinsky took a few friends to dinner at an exclusive French restaurant. He ordered a bottle of wine. The waiter informed him that he was mispronouncing the name of the wine. "It is Châteauneuf-du-Pape," said the waiter. Belinsky looked up from his drink, his eyebrows raised inquisitively. "Oh, it is, is it?" And then he picked up the table, which was loaded with shrimp cocktails and bread sticks, and threw it through a window.

Eventually, events so turned on Belinsky that even Mamie Van Doren became disillusioned with her "Bo."

One day she announced tearfully to a host of reporters that Bo and she were terminating their engagement. "I'm returning his ring," she said. "I'm afraid if I don't he'll cut off my finger and take it—or worse, make me take over the payments." Belinsky's response was characteristic. "Mamie's a good broad," he said to the press. "I still think she's got a little class—very little."

Despite growing public disenchantment with his behavior, Belinsky was undaunted. He denied that his acts were those of an unstable man. "I feel I'm very stable," he told a sportswriter. "Proof of which is that I'm still single. Only unstable guys get married." Shortly after that remark, Belinsky married Jo Collins, a *Playboy* playmate. That marriage ended prematurely one night when Belinsky tore a $500 wig from his wife's head and threw it onto Sunset Strip. "It just goes to show," he said afterwards, "you can't play hearts and flowers with a product of nudity."

Finally, on his thirtieth birthday, four years before he would retire unnoticed from baseball, Bo Belinsky admitted publicly that his once-promising career had ceased to exist. (At the time he was struggling with a 1-5 record for the Houston Astros.) His career had collapsed, he said, under the weight of too many fines, suspensions, trades and banishments to the minors—not to mention the weight of his own personality. And it seemed, he added, that each setback was visited upon him just as he was about to reach his peak, until now, at 30, there were no more peaks in sight. He also admitted that his public, which had found him an entertaining enough young man as a winner, had grown increasingly weary of, and finally annoyed with, what it felt was unstable and self-destructive behavior. As an aging and unsuccessful playboy, Bo Belinsky had become a parody of himself.

When a Houston sportswriter asked him how sport's most notorious playboy felt upon reaching 30, Bo replied with a smile. "Babe, it's no fun knowing that in every home in America your birthday is celebrated as a day of infamy." An exaggeration, perhaps, for it is doubtful whether anyone in America, including Belinsky himself, celebrated his birthday at all. However, that remark was telling. It was characteristically clever—one might say almost too clever. It seemed to have been delivered more for affect than truth by a man more concerned with style than substance. It was tossed off, discarded really, with an ironic smile of disavowal, as if to say it was nothing but the surplus from a warehouse of such remarks, remarks its author must unload whenever he felt the occasion deserved. Despite all this, one still had the annoying suspicion that Bo Belinsky felt his remark contained more truth than wit. It was not clear whether this feeling was the overblown self-pity of a too-shallow man or the heightened perception of a too-sensitive man. It was only clear that Robert "Bo" Belinsky had dissipated a promising career, that his public had grown weary of him and that much of his difficulty could be traced to his personality. It seemed he did not have the knack of such later athletes —the Namaths, Harrelsons, and Sandersons—of consciously cultivating his personality precisely up to, but not beyond, that point at which the public becomes bored with it.

Bo Belinsky, 35 years old, leans forward in his armchair to better examine the picture of himself holding that no-hit baseball of nine years past. With his fingertips he displaces a lock of hair from his forehead. It is an exquisite, almost delicate gesture done in slow motion. His hair is black. He wears it long and shaggy rather than slicked back and gleaming as he did nine years ago. Its blackness, coupled with his tanned skin and slightly flattened features, gives him the appearance of a man of Mexican descent. He is still darkly handsome, although his skin is no longer tight and sleek. There are small lines at the corners of his eyes and mouth. He is wearing only a cream-colored bathing suit with the word "Bo" scripted above the left leg.

He looks to be about 6-1 and 190 pounds—a gain of 10 pounds over the years. And yet, despite the added flesh spilling over the waist of his trunks, despite the tiny stubble of beard and the lines and the look of aging, somehow Bo Belinsky looks better than he did nine years ago. He looks truer, more substantial, as if the lines and added weight had forced upon him dimensions and substance he did not have nine years ago, and which he had not consciously cultivated since. He looks less slick, less glossy, less conscious of his external self. He no longer possesses that pampered, self-satisfied look that gave one the impression that if you tried to grab hold of him your hands would slip off with the grease.

After his no-hitter his mother told reporters that her son worked out every day in a gym. "Bo just loves his body," she said. Today, a hot summer morning six months after his retirement from baseball, Bo Belinsky no longer "works out." As is his custom, he will do nothing more strenuous than sit for hours in the living room of this spacious ranch house tucked high into the Hollywood Hills overlooking Los Angeles. Possibly he will work out his horoscope. He is a Sagittarius. ("The most flexible sign in the universe," he says. "A Sag gets along with everyone.") But it makes little difference what his day's horoscope suggests (a long hike in the mountains?), for his routine will not vary. He will sit until noon in the shadow of the chimney centered in the living room so as to best avoid the sunlight pouring through the sliding glass doors to his left. He will sip steadily from the glass on the coffee table beside his armchair and, to amuse himself, will watch a morning quiz show; or answer the constantly ringing telephone; or just gaze at the many paintings, poems, camp artifacts and photographs that litter the walls. Most of the photographs are of his friends, some in cowboy suits with drawn guns and pixy smiles, others bearded, with windblown hair and glazed, meditative looks. Throughout the day Belinsky will pass the time in an endless stream of gossip and small talk with those same friends who will drift into and out of this room over which he presides, the orchestrator of the day's unfolding.

It is nine o'clock in the morning and the room is occupied by about seven or eight people in various states of sprawl. All are strangely quiet, self-contained, as if this huge room was a universe and each person in it a planet unto himself, spinning in an orbit entirely his own. Most of them, including Belinsky, have yet to get to sleep after last night's party, which concluded only minutes ago.

To Belinsky's left on the other side of the coffee table sits a pudgy, gray-haired little man in his 50s. He is wearing striped bellbottoms and no shirt. His name is Phil. He works for a company that makes locks and burglar alarms. ("I've been trying to get him to give me the combinations," says Belinsky. "What a score, eh?") Phil is bent forward, his elbows on his knees, his face buried in his hands. He is moaning softly. Beside his chair, folded like a jacknife on the couch, sits a tall, slender girl in a flowered bikini. Bonnie is about 18, maybe 17. She has the face of a young Sophia Loren. Her chin is resting on her raised knee so she can best paint her toenails with complete self-absorption. Occasionally she will look up, wide-eyed, and blow a kiss in Belinsky's direction. He will smile back. ("A stray," he says. "I found her last night on the Strip. She says she wants to stay." He shrugs.)

Another girl in a flowered bikini is moving languidly about the room, collecting glasses, emptying ashtrays, dusting. She is older than Bonnie, maybe 30, but also tall and cool. She is not quite so pretty. Linda has pale blue eyes, bright red hair and a fleshy, but attractive, body. She, too, seems self-absorbed as she works, only her self-absorption seems less single-minded than does Bonnie's. ("Linda's a good chickie," says Bo. "She's got her share of patches.")

To the left of the couch, standing in front of the mirror above the leather-padded bar, is a small, lean man in his

161

late 30s. He has fine, straight features, unblinking eyes, a long ponytail and gray muttonchop sideburns. He is studiously fluffing out his sideburns with one hand, while with the other he adjusts the cartridge belt slung over one shoulder. His name is Chris. He is a prophet. Every afternoon at lunchtime he walks down to Schwab's drugstore on Sunset Strip, climbs onto a soap box and, with his German shepherd panting beside him, preaches to the passersby. Today he will warn them that if they continue to worship material things they will never be able to see spiritual things. "Dead things are for blind people," he will say. And then, "The jackals of hell will lick your blood from the streets." Then he will walk back to the house, prepare an organic lunch for himself and his dog and watch "The Dating Game" on television. Sometimes he watches the news. But when he does he invariably ends up arguing with one of the commentators. It is not an uncommon sight to walk into the living room and see Chris standing with his finger poked at an image of David Brinkley, who is laconically reading from a paper as Chris shouts at him, "Distorter of facts! Harbinger of doom! Tool of corrupt establishments!" (Bo says of Chris, "He's all right. A little freaky, maybe, but aren't we all? He's got his little act, so what? Everybody's got a little act.")

To Chris's right, alongside the glass sliding doors that overlook a tear-shaped swimming pool one story below, a skinny little man in a white bathing suit is sleeping on a wall couch. Awake, he is skittish, quick-witted, caustic. His name is Len and he owns this house in which Belinsky is staying. ("Len's a gas," says Belinsky. "He's the unofficial mayor of Los Angeles.") Len's presence on the couch is making it difficult for the painter to reach the wall behind him. The painter has been painting that same wall for six days. Every so often he pauses and glances out the glass doors at the swimming pool below. Two girls are sunning themselves beside the pool. They are both lying on their backs, each with the back of a hand flattened across her eyes. Both girls are wearing only the bottoms of their bikinis. ("He went freaky the first time he looked out that window," says Belinsky of the painter. "He's been painting that same wall ever since. I think we'll send *him* a bill!")

At about noon Belinsky and his friends, some of whom are sleeping in other rooms throughout the house, will join those two girls beside the pool. Belinsky will sit by the pool "taking some color" until one of his friends sneaks up behind him and pushes him into the pool, or until he feels sweat seeping from his body, in which case he will dive in to cool himself, emerging quickly and returning to his deck chair. But noon is still hours away.

Belinsky puts down the picture of himself and sits back in his chair. "What was I thinking then?" he says. "I was thinking, 'Man, a no-hitter, that's nice! I wonder what happens next?' I mean, a no-hitter, it's nice but it's no big thing." He picks up his glass, takes a sip and returns it to the table. "Sure, I would have liked to have had a career after that. But I never thought I would. I knew there's always someone waiting around the corner to take a shot at you. It's just a matter of time. Besides, there's no way I could have done anything different—I mean, lived my life differently. Can a leopard change his spots? You can shave

163

all the fur off the poor bastard and he's still got his spots, right? Who can explain it? Why does a mad dog howl at the moon? Why did I do the things I did?" He smiles, picks up his glass and drains it. He motions with it toward the tall redhead who has been tidying up. "Heh, Babe, some more Wheaties?"

Linda looks up from her dusting. "Sure, Bo." She moves to his chair and bends over to take his glass. Her breasts strain against the top of her bikini. Bo looks up, shakes his head once. "All right, Babe! That's all right!" Linda, poised over him, looks down at her breasts and then to Belinsky. They both smile, that identical, knowing, self-mocking smile. Linda takes his glass and straightens up. She tosses her long red hair from her eyes and laughs a noiseless laugh that comes in spurts, like breaths. "Bo, you're too much," she says. She turns her back on him and moves off in a languid, loose-hipped shuffle. Belinsky follows her with his eyes, shaking his head and saying, "So many broads, man, so many broads. It's a shame . . . heh, what's that poem, 'Give me ten stouthearted men, and soon I'll have ten thousand more.' Well, make mine chickies. Yes sir, make mine chickies," and he laughs. He slides down into his chair, only the top of his head visible, and he laughs.

When his laughter fades he is silent for a while, smiling to himself. Absentmindedly he begins curling a lock of hair at the back of his head. Finally he says, "My problem was simple, Babe. I heard music nobody else heard." As he speaks he is staring straight ahead at the chimney. "I remember once I was playing in the Texas League when

164

the team bus stopped in Veracruz so we could eat. All the players went into the restaurant except me. I thought I heard music down the street so I went looking for it. I found a two-piece jazz band playing on the sidewalk in front of a bar. I listened for a while, and when they went inside I followed them. I had a few drinks and then I left. I had every intention of returning to that bus until I ran into another jazz band down the street. I followed them into a bar too. What I didn't know was that all these bars hired jazz bands to lure customers inside. Man, after that bar, it seemed like every step I took there were these damned buglers waiting just for me. 'Here he comes!' they seemed to be saying. 'Get ready, here he comes!' . . . I woke up six days later in a hotel room in Acapulco. I had a sponsor. This blonde Mexican broad—she had to be blonde, right!—was sitting by the bed saying, 'Belinsky! Belinsky! I make you great Yanqui bullfighter! But first we must change your name.' I said, 'Sure, Babe. We'll change it to Lance. Lance Belinsky, how's that?' . . . My team? They were in Mexico City. We passed each other going in opposite directions. It was always like that with me."

It is 10 o'clock now. The sun has begun to move from behind the chimney into Belinsky's path. It streams in through the glass doors and momentarily blinds him. He raises one hand to shade his eyes. With the other he searches across the coffee table for his sunglasses. When he finds them he puts them on. "That's better," he says. "Too much sun. Too much . . . ." Then suddenly he says, "I don't feel sorry for myself. No way. I knew sooner or later I'd have to pay the piper. You can't beat the piper,

Babe. I never thought I could. But I'll tell you who I do feel sorry for." He leans over the arm of his chair, furtively looking left and right as if afraid the others will eavesdrop on this secret he is about to impart. A meaningless gesture. They are oblivious to him. Satisfied no one is listening, he turns and says softly, "I feel sorry for all those poor bastards who never heard music." He laughs out loud. "Those poor fucking bastards!" and he falls back into his chair laughing.

The doorbell rings. Linda, returning with Bo's drink, goes to the door. It is the telephone repairman. Linda leads him to the glass doors overlooking the pool. The painter sighs disgustedly, as if severely hampered in his work by this crush of people about him. He begins feverishly slapping the wall with his brush. Linda points down at the swimming pool. The telephone repairman looks down for a very long moment. Then he looks at Linda.

"How did they get in the swimming pool?" he says.

Linda shrugs. "There was a call for Lloyd Bridges," and she walks over to Belinsky and hands him his drink.

"A call for Lloyd Bridges?" Bo repeats. "That's trippy, Babe. That's real trippy." He takes his glass, raises it before his eyes and says with a smile, "To amnesia." He sips delicately, then puts the glass on the table. He picks up a book of famous quotations and begins flipping through the pages. He is looking for the source of the quotation, 'Give me ten stouthearted men. . . .'

Meanwhile, the telephone man has found the sockets out of which the two white telephones had been removed. He looks over his shoulder and says to no one in particular, "The phones were ripped out of the wall."

Belinsky looks over at him, his eyebrows raised, and says, "Is that a fact, Babe? Ripped out, huh?" He shakes his head in disbelief and goes back to his book. It was Belinsky who had removed the telephones from the wall only hours ago. When he had come home from an all-night party he had been met at the door by Phil, who told him he'd been kept awake all night long answering calls from such friends of Bo's as Hollywood Mike, Chicago Danny and Red-Headed Mike.

"A new arrangement must be worked out with the telephones," said Phil.

Belinsky replied, "Sure, Babe," and walked over to the telephones, ripped them out of the wall and threw them through the sliding glass doors (which, fortunately, were opened) into the deepest part of the swimming pool.

It was not Belinsky's disagreement with Phil that precipitated his outburst, however. Its seeds had been sown much earlier in the evening when Bo, Len and three male friends had begun their nightly rounds of Sunset Strip nightclubs. They stopped first at a favorite haunt just as three of that club's exotic dancers, dressed only in their nightgowns, were being ushered into a police car. The girls' arrest stemmed from an act they had just performed on stage while three crew-cut members of the L.A. vice squad watched from a darkened corner table. The act centered around one girl who took a bath on stage and was soon joined in her tub by the other two who washed her back. "It's a helluva act," said Belinsky as the police car drove off.

Disappointed but undaunted, Belinsky and his party went on to The Sportspage, a hangout for professional athletes, and then on to The Candy Store, a Beverly Hills discotheque frequented by Hollywood celebrities. At both places Belinsky's party was virtually ignored. They were seated at darkened tables far removed from the action. Belinsky himself went essentially unrecognized except for two isolated incidents. At The Sportspage he was approached by a pot-bellied man who wanted him to play on his Sunday morning softball team. "A great way to stay in shape," said the man. "We have free beer after the game." At The Candy Store Belinsky was approached by a gray-haired man dressed entirely in white, like Tom Mix, who said he was a movie producer who wanted to make a film of Belinsky's life.

"I have just the title," said Belinsky. "We'll call it, 'A Funny Thing Happened on the Way to a Career.'"

The man in white said, "That's good, Bo. That's very, very good. Maybe you can play yourself. Can you act?"

"Have I got an act!" replied Belinsky.

At about midnight Belinsky and his friends got up to leave The Candy Store. Len pointed to a man leaning against the wall near the doorway. "Catch his act," said Len. "He's doing an imitation of Hugh Hefner." The man had chalky-white skin. He was wearing a purple velvet jumpsuit and smoking a pipe. His arms were folded across his chest as if he were hugging himself. His act turned out not to be an act, however, and after a few words of greeting Hugh Hefner invited Belinsky and as many friends as he could muster to a party at his Beverly Hills mansion.

"I'm bored tonight," said Hefner as he led Belinsky and Len to his Rolls Royce. "Barbie's in the hospital and I could use some company."

By the time Hugh Hefner's black limousine reached the electronically controlled gate that opened to a winding driveway that led eventually to his $3.5 million Tudor castle, it was being trailed by nearly a dozen Fords, Chevys and Pontiacs of various age and hue. The cars were filled with about 30 casual friends of Belinsky, most of whom were small-time hustlers and gamblers operating along Sunset Strip.

The party at the Elizabethan castle began at 2 A.M., with Hefner leading his guests on a tour of his possessions. He showed them his gleaming kitchen where his cooks (like all his servants, on 24-hour call) were preparing a snack for them. He showed them his bed, his game room, his projection room, his vast, neatly clipped grounds discriminantly dotted with intimate little lovers' parks. And finally he showed them his as yet uncompleted swimming pool, which was the size of a small lake. Because the pool was nothing more than a huge dirt- and boulder-strewn ditch, Hefner led his guests back inside where he produced an architect's drawing of the finished product. The pool would eventually resemble one of those lush jungle hideaways seen so often on men's after-shave commercials on television. It would be planted with overhanging tropical foliage and tanned, bikini'd bunnies. (The bunnies were

169

shown in various poses—lying on a rock, sunning their already brown bodies, one knee languorously raised.)

When Hefner had shown his guests all the possessions he felt they should see, he led them to the living room, where his servants had spread out a snack of red and black caviar, strawberries and melon, assorted cheeses and bottles of champagne. By then his guests had grown ravenous with hunger—only their hunger was not for the food surrounding them but for the opulent life-style they had just devoured with their eyes. Their quick hustlers' minds clicked into gear. They searched frantically for a way, as Belinsky put it, "To hitch a ride on that big bunny bird in the sky." The men began talking loudly about "deals" and "scores" they could make if only they had the proper "backing." The women, urged on by their boyfriends, passed behind Hefner and stooped to whisper in his ear about "deals" of their own, about "scores" they had in mind—such as being able to stencil across their navals tomorrow morning, "Property of Hugh Hefner Enterprises."

"It was an orgy," said Belinsky afterwards. "Everyone was climbing each others' back to buzz in Hefner's ear."

Throughout the frenzy, however, Hefner remained impassive. He sat Indian-style on a velvet pillow on the floor, his guests spread out before him. His arms were folded across his chest; his pipe alternately dangled from one hand or was clenched between his teeth; his small black eyes darted from guest to guest, the eyes reading but unreadable. He did not say more than a dozen words all morning (as if somehow his daily allotment had been exhausted on his guided tour), but instead contented himself with watching the anguished strivings of those about him. Like some voyeur of human anxieties, he seemed to actually take pleasure in the sweaty brows and clenched stomachs of his guests. Throughout the morning his head bobbed forward mechanically, like a string puppet's, although it bobbed not in approval to the words of his guests (as they mistakenly believed) but in silent affirmation to some private truth he took great pleasure in seeing verified before his eyes.

From a distant corner of the room, seated alone, Belinsky watched the proceedings silently. As the morning wore on he grew sullen. Unsure of the source of his anger, he began to drink heavily. At dawn he saw Hefner stand up suddenly, thank his guests for coming and leave the room. The guests looked dazedly at each other. Then, half-drunk, half-asleep, unsure of what next was expected of them, they rose unsteadily and began to wander out of the house into a chill and foggy morning.

When Belinsky and Len returned to Len's house in Hollywood Hills, Phil met Bo at the door and complained about the telephones. "What followed," said Len with a grin, "was a typical Polack rage."

Belinsky puts down the book of quotations and says, "Going to Hefner's house was no big thing for me. I've known the guy for years. He offered me a job, but I turned it down. I never went much for that Playboy philosophy and stuff. I'm not one for institutionalized sex. I mean, you don't use women, Babe, you compliment them. They compliment you. How can you use a woman? We all

171

climbed out of a womb, right? But still, Heff's a gracious host. I wanted my friends to enjoy themselves last night. It was a score for them, something they could talk about for a week. Instead, they tried to hock his silverware. The stupid bastards!"

Bo sips from his glass, then sips again, and finally says with raised eyebrows, "I met my wife through Heff. She's one reason I quit baseball. I've got this thing going with her, a divorce action. It's no big thing but it started to get me down a little. I haven't done much these past months except try to get amnesia." He raises his glass and smiles. "But it was my own fault. Some guys love to get their dummy knocked by a broad. And to top it off, she's a Leo. Man, those Leo broads are very tough. Very self-righteous. Always reminding you of how *you* blew it. Ha! As if you needed reminding! I split finally when she said she wanted to be a bunny den mother at the Playboy Club in Denver. How's that, Babe, trippy? A bunny mother? What'd that make me, a bunny daddy?"

While Bo speaks, the room and its occupants remain essentially unchanged. It is now 11 A.M. Len is still sleeping by the glass doors while the painter and telephone repairman work around him. Linda is still tidying up in that floating, ethereal way of hers. Phil is still moaning into his hands. Bonnie is still painting her toenails. Chris, the prophet, is the only person to have altered his orbit. He is sitting cross-legged on the floor, leafing through pages of notes he will use for this afternoon's sermon at Schwab's drugstore. Satisfied, Chris reaches for the one available telephone Belinsky somehow missed in his earlier rage, and begins dialing. He asks the operator to put him through to Secretary of State Rogers. "In Washington, D.C.," he adds. Belinsky stops talking and motions toward Chris with his glass. He raises a finger to his lips and in an exaggerated manner cocks an ear. Chris tells the operator he is trying to locate the sacred Hopi burial grounds. "It's somewhere in the Mojave desert," he says. "The Secretary would know. What? This is Chris. Tell him Chris is calling."

Belinsky shakes his head and laughs silently to himself. He sips the last of his drink and then shakes the glass so the ice cubes tinkle. Linda looks over and nods. Bo does not begin talking again until Linda returns with another full glass.

"My wife wasn't the only reason I quit," he says. "You could say I no longer heard 'The Tunes of Glory.' I never liked baseball that much, at first anyway. I only signed a contract to get out of Trenton. Things were getting a little tacky for me there. I was hustling pool and hanging around with some bad people. At the time $185 a month and a ticket to some witches' monastery in Pancakesville, Ga., didn't look so bad. I quit baseball a number of times over the years, but for one reason or another I always came back. I almost quit in the spring of 1962. The Angels wanted me to sign a standard rookie contract and I refused. Then a few months later I pitched the no-hitter. The rest is history. I threatened to quit a few times after that no-hitter, like when they shipped me to Hawaii for hitting that sportswriter. It was like they were sending me into

173

exile. I felt disconnected from things, so I threatened to quit. But that was just a bluff on my part.

"There was no way I could quit. I had learned to love the game by then. That's funny, isn't it, Babe? Me, the guy everybody said didn't love the game enough. Ha! I ended up devoting 15 years of my life to baseball. Man, I loved the fucking game. I just didn't take it seriously, that's all. I mean, Babe, I don't take myself seriously, how could I take a game seriously. It's just a game for little boys. To play it you've got to be a little boy at heart. The problem is some of these apples—you know, jocks—take it too seriously. They let the game define them. They become, say, a great hitter, and they begin to think of themselves as great in ways that have nothing to do with their baseball talent. They define themselves in ways they aren't. They get a little act and they take it all so fucking seriously.

"I never let any game define me. I was serious when I pitched, but once off that mound I defined myself. So what if I loved a few broads or took a drink? That didn't make me a bad guy, did it? I tried to live my life the way I wanted, with a little style, a little creativity. In the long run it wore me down, physically and mentally. Not the playing around, but fighting those bastards who misunderstood me. The apples said I was bad for the game. My managers were always trying to straighten me out. They'd call me into their office and try to read my act. You know, 'Come on, kid, what seems to be bothering you? You can tell me, I'm on your side.' And when I opened up, when I stood there with my insides hanging out, they buttoned

174

themselves up. The next day they'd run to the front office and I'd get shipped to the minors again. Those bastards! They wouldn't pull dead rats off their own mothers!"

He takes a sip from his glass, calms himself and then continues. "It was then I realized this wasn't a man's game. Men chase broads and get drunk and are straight with you. They don't have an act. They aren't hypocrites. For example, when I was going with Mamie they called me into the office every day and told me she was no good for me. Finally, when I wouldn't listen, they shipped my ass to Hawaii. And while I'm there I get this call from Mamie telling me that the same front office people who shipped me out were trying to rip her off while I'm gone." He smiles and nods his head. "Is that trippy or isn't it? . . . If only I didn't see that shit I would have been all right. But I had this goddamned third eye, and when I saw things I shouldn't have I overreacted. Usually it was in a way that made no sense, like getting drunk or something. Maybe I'm too sensitive. Maybe I see things out of proportion, or things that aren't even there. Maybe I just don't know how to express what I feel. Who knows? You tell me, Babe. You're my Doctor. . . .

"Anyway, I always felt the front office and the manager and the players should be one big family. They shouldn't take sides against each other. Man, you live part of your life with these people. They are, in a sense, your family. The owner should be like a father to you, take care of you, protect you. Take my last year at Cincinnati [1970]. Everybody knew I was on the way out. So why didn't the bastards start me one game, just one last game? Why couldn't

175

they let me go out in style instead of letting me rot on the bench? Or the Angels. The fucking Angels! They had an old-timers' game recently and they didn't even invite me. I wouldn't have gone if they did, but Jesus, Babe, they've got my glove and spikes in their Hall of Fame! I pitched the first no-hitter in California major league history! I did it before Koufax or Marichal or any of those fuckers."

Bonnie, who has finished her toenails, stands up suddenly and yawns. She looks down at her toes and wiggles them. "How do they look, Bo?" she says. Belinsky looks at her, open-mouthed, stunned. "What, Babe?"

"My toes, Bo! How do they look?" She wiggles them again.

Belinsky shakes his head wearily and then smiles. "Babe, they look beautiful. Really beautiful."

Bonnie, satisfied, looks around the room, sighs and says, "Bo, there's nothing to do. I'm bored."

"Why don't you read a book, Babe?"

"Oh, Bo, I can't stand still long enough to read a book. Maybe I should go swimming."

"Sure, Babe, that's it." Then he points to the painter and adds in a whisper, "Go topless. It'll freak him out."

Bonnie purses her lips and says, "Bo, you're terrible!" She walks out of the room, her hands contorted behind her back unhooking the top of her bikini.

"She's some chickie, isn't she?" says Belinsky. "All she needs is a little silicone and I'll have to call up Heff." He laughs. "About a ton of silicone." He sinks back into his chair and begins cracking his knuckles. He is staring straight ahead at the chimney, which he seems not to see. His eyes pass through and beyond a picture of Len in a full-faced beard. Len's picture is superimposed over a poem that reads: "The drifter has vanished/The dreamer, with age, has gone blind."

Belinsky turns suddenly and leans over the arm of his chair, the room reflected in concave miniature in his dark glasses. "You know, I played 15 years of baseball and never made a dime off it. I wasn't that interested in success, that's why. I loved the game, Babe, not success. Most ball-players are whores at heart. Do you think Seaver or Ken Harrelson play the game because they love it? You bet your ass they don't. They love what it brings them, Babe. I could never give up enough of myself for success.

"Len Schecter approached me about a baseball exposé long before he ever hooked onto Jim Bouton. I told him I wasn't interested. I couldn't rat on guys I'd played with, even if they were bastards. That's not my style. I was the last of baseball's true sportsmen. My heart was in the game—the game, the fucking game, that's all. I never stashed baseball. You know what I mean? Stash! Stash! Stash!" He stands up and thrusts his hand down his leg as if into his pants pocket. He repeats the gesture again, again, again, while saying, "You can't stash 'sport'. Those other bastards talk about 'sport' and they mean 'business,' they mean something they can stash in their pockets. Man, you can't stash baseball. If you're lucky, you capture it awhile, you go through it at some point in your life and then it goes away and you go on to something else. Some guys try to live off it forever. Babe, it's a sin to live off 'sport.' "

Belinsky sits down again. He is quiet for a moment, trying to compose himself. Then he says softly, but in measured tones, "I mean, baseball is a beautiful thing. It's clean. It stays the same. It's an equalizer. It moves slowly in a time when everything around us is rushing like mad. It's a . . . gee, what am I trying to say. It's a breath of fresh air blowing across the country. Don't laugh, I mean it! Listen, during World War II when those Jap kamikaze pilots flew down the smokestacks of our ships, do you know what they screamed? 'Fuck Babe Ruth!' That's right, 'Fuck Babe Ruth!' Not 'Fuck Knute Rockne!' or 'Fuck Bronco Nagurski!' but 'Fuck Babe Ruth!' That's the way I feel about the game, even today. I just never knew how to express myself properly, that's all. I loved the game, but I love it my way, not the way people told me I should love it.

"I owe baseball. It kept me straight. Who knows what I might have been without it. Baseball was the one big thing in my life—if my life contained any big thing. My running around with broads, that was just passing time. It was baseball that mattered. I mean, Sport keeps you clean, but only for a while. In the long run it isn't even Sport that matters, it's you. You've got to know when to get off or else you start handing out too many transfers."

Belinsky reaches down for his glass, picks it up, then, without taking a sip, returns it to the table. "Take this house," he says with a sweeping gesture of his arm. "I'm just a guest here. No matter where I've been or who I've been with, I've always been just a guest. I like it that way. I'm like camouflage. I blend in anywhere—but not for too long. Pretty soon I think I'll head for the Islands. If I stand around here too long I'll kill the grass. That's the

way I've set up my life. I don't want to take root anywhere. You hear about good soil here or there and you're
curious, but really you're afraid to find it. I mean, Babe,
you take root, you give your trust to someone, and it's
bound to fall apart. I don't want to be around when
things fall apart. I'm more spiritual than people think. I
don't do malice to anyone. I don't like to see people hurt.
When I sense things are falling apart—I have this radar—
I snap alert, and then I'm gone. Follow the sun, Babe.
That's it, I follow the sun. . . . I hate it, this way I am.
But who chooses to be what he is, huh? It's in the stars,
Babe, in the stars. I would like to be devoted to someone
or something. . . . I just never found anything I could lend
myself to. The age of chivalry is dead, Babe. There are no
more heroes."

He smiles and stands up. "Nothing left worthy of devo-
tion, know what I mean? That's why my way is best. Don't
forget, 'He who plays and runs away, lives to play some
other day.' " He throws his head back and laughs, that
self-mocking laugh. Then he holds up his empty glass and
says, "Excuse me, Babe. I need more Wheaties. Besides,
this conversation is getting a little heavy. Too heavy." He
laughs again as he moves off. "Too heavy, Babe." He
moves with a long and graceful stride, his body shifting
delicately from side to side, his weight slightly forward on
the balls of his feet. And yet he moves so lightly, ever so
lightly, a man on hot coals, a cat about to spring or flee,
leaving not the slightest indentation on this thick carpet
over which he passes.

A Jouster with Windmills

He searches the hotel room for a round object. Finding none, he picks up an ashtray from the table beside his bed. "Imagine this a baseball," he says. The ashtray is black. It is made of cut glass and it is square. He grips the ashtray in his right hand as if it is a baseball. His first two fingers and thumb encircle three sides of the square perimeter. His other two fingers are knuckled under its base. "Now, to break off a real fine curveball," he says, "you have to turn your wrist like this here." He holds the ashtray at eye level about a foot and a half in front of him. His right arm is not quite fully extended. He tilts the ashtray upright so that his first two fingers are on top, his thumb below, and he is looking directly into its scooped-out center. He holds the ashtray as if it is a small camera through which he is sighting, although it is too far away. Now he begins to rotate his wrist very slowly so that his top fingers move away from him and down, and his thumb moves toward him and up. Soon the ashtray is level, as it was when resting on the table. His hand is cocked as if the ashtray is a pistol he is aiming; his thumb closest to him, his first two fingers farthest away. He continues to rotate his wrist in this direction until the ashtray has turned 180 degrees from its original position and he is staring directly at its base. The original position of his fingers and thumb has been reversed too, and now his thumb is on top and his first two fingers on the bottom.

"See," he says, "it's a very simple, natural motion." He repeats the whole procedure, only this time he rotates the ashtray in a more fluid, sweeping manner so that as his wrist turns he is simultaneously drawing that ashtray into his chest. Again it's all done in perfect slow motion, very gracefully, almost with tenderness, as one might draw a beautiful woman to one's chest.

"It *is* a natural motion," he says in soft wonder. "It's real easy and natural." He repeats it again and again and again, each time drawing that woman to his chest until it is apparent that his repetition is only in small part for his student's sake, and more for his own. With each repetition he seems to be reaffirming the clarity and logic of that motion, and he takes great pleasure in each reaffirmation. As he repeats that motion, over and over and over, he speaks in a soothing drawl, that opiate that softens resistance, that makes one helplessly open and receptive to his teaching. It is as if one was asleep while the recording of a foreign language played over and over, until, upon waking, one discovered he has learned a new language. Only it is not really learned, not acquired consciously, but rather absorbed as if through osmosis. And it is absorbed so effortlessly that it seems not so new after all. It becomes something natural one has possessed all along, although buried, and for which this teacher deserves credit only for nudging to the surface. And then this new possession—rather, this old possession newly discovered—becomes in one's own mind one's very own in a way nothing learned can ever be.

He stops, puts the ball in his left hand and says, "If you throw it right the ball should break something like this here." He cups his now empty right hand and draws a backward *S* in the air. "See, it goes away from a batter and down at the same time." He draws another backward *S*, then another and another, each one drawn gracefully, with care, the shape of that beautiful but elusive woman he has committed to memory. He takes the ball in his right hand and, standing beside his bed, he begins his motion. He is wearing a pale blue shirt, a dark blue tie and navy flared slacks. He pumps, reaches back, kicks, moves forward and at the last possible second pulls that woman to his chest.

John Franklin Sain, the 53-year-old pitching coach of the Chicago White Sox, is a big man, almost 6-3 and over 200 pounds. He has one of those thin men's builds that with age takes on weight through the chest and arms while the legs remain thin. His face is small-featured, leathery, creased, and his checks are lumpy from years of chewing tobacco. He would look to be a very gruff man, without tenderness, if not for his smile, which is faint, and his eyes, which are a clear, youthful blue. That smile (not a smile, really, just a show of teeth) and those eyes (wincing, vaguely distant) lend him the air of a man perpetually scanning the horizon for uncertain shapes and shadows, quite possibly for windmills, whose presence he is sure of but whose form escapes him.

When Johnny Sain became the White Sox pitching coach in the spring of 1971 he inherited a staff that had recorded the highest earned-run average (4.54), had allowed the most hits (1554), had given up the most home runs (164) and had been touched for the most runs (822) of all 12 American League teams in 1970. The White Sox finished last in team pitching in the American League. Their most successful pitcher was seven-year veteran Tommy John, who won 12 games and lost 17. Under Sain's tutelage in 1971 the White Sox finished fourth in the American League in team pitching and fifth overall. The staff ERA was 3.12. The Sox placed three pitchers in the top 15 of the American League; produced one 22-game winner, journeyman knuckleballer Wilbur Wood, who had won a little over twice that many games in his previous eight years in the majors; and unveiled two of the game's brightest new prospects in Tom Bradley, a rookie, who won 15 games and posted a 2.96 ERA, and Bart Johnson, who won 12 games with an ERA of 2.93. As a team the White Sox finished third in their Western Division after having finished dead last a year before, and there was much speculation that the club's rookie manager, Chuck Tanner, might be voted the American League's Manager of the Year.

Before coming to the White Sox, Sain was the minor

league pitching coach for the California Angels in 1970. It was there that he met Chuck Tanner, then the manager of the Angels' Pacific Coast League team, Hawaii. At that time Sain also first noticed Tom Bradley and another present-day White Sox youngster, Steve Kealey, also a pitcher. "This is the second year I've worked with Johnny Sain," says Kealey. "When I was in spring training with the Angels I only talked to him once. The Angels' front office wouldn't let any big-leaguers talk to him. They told us to stay away from Sain."

Before going to the Angels, Johnny Sain had been the major league pitching coach of the Detroit Tigers from 1967 to 1969, when he was fired. During those years Denny McLain won 31 games and 25 games in successive seasons; after Sain left Detroit, McLain managed to lose as many as 22 games. Earl Wilson won 22 games under Johnny Sain, the only time in his 11-year major league career he was a 20-game winner. Mickey Lolich, although only a 19-game winner under Sain, became a 25-game winner shortly after Sain left Detroit. "Johnny Sain made me a 20-game winner," says Lolich today. "Without his help I never would have done it."

Before going to Detroit, Sain was the pitching coach of the Minnesota Twins from 1965 to 1966, when he was fired. During those years Mudcat Grant and Jim Kaat became 20-game winners for the first and only times in their careers, and Dave Boswell and Jim Perry improved so much that they would become 20-game winners shortly after Sain left the Twins.

Before going to the Twins, Sain had been the pitching

185

coach of the New York Yankees from 1961 to 1963, when he was not fired but simply was not rehired by the team's new general manager, Ralph Houk. While Sain coached, Yankee pitchers Jim Bouton, Ralph Terry and Whitey Ford became 20-game winners for the only times in their careers. Ford won 66 games and lost only 19 in his three years under Sain; Ralph Terry won 56 games in three years with Sain, which was more than half as many games as he had won in his 12-year career. Jim Bouton won 21 games under Sain, and when Sain left the club in 1963 Bouton said of him, "I admire Johnny Sain more than any man I've ever met."

Sain began his coaching career in 1959 with the Kansas City Athletics, where he worked with, among others, Dick Drago, who was then a minor-leaguer but today is one of baseball's better pitchers. Prior to his first coaching venture Sain had been an outstanding relief pitcher with the powerful New York Yankees of the 1950s. In 1951 he won only two games at the tail end of the season, but they were such crucial victories, putting the Yankees into the World Series, that his teammates voted him a full World Series share. In 1952 Sain was 11 and 6 as a relief pitcher, and the next year he was 14 and 7. The Yankees won the pennant and the World Series in both years.

But Johnny Sain's reputation as an astute major league pitcher was not built in the Fifties, but in the Forties, when, with Warren Spahn, he was a perennial 20-game winner for the Boston Braves. From 1946 to 1950 Johnny Sain won 20 or more games in one season four times. Spahn did it three times. The two men accomplished their

186

feats with such apparent ease (Sain threw the last pitch in his first 48 major league victories) that their rabid Boston fans deified them.

Johnny Sain, a native of Havana, Ark., a tiny hamlet at the foot of the Ozark mountains, signed his first professional baseball contract for the sum of $50 per month with Troy, Ala., of the Class D Cotton State League at the age of 18. After one pitching appearance, in which he was shelled unmercifully, he was given his unconditional release. Within the next three years Sain would be released by three other minor league teams, all of which felt he did not have sufficient speed to become a major league pitcher. One major league scout watched Sain pitch a shutout and then wrote his front office, saying he hadn't seen a ballplayer on the field. In fact, Sain himself never had "the wildest dream" he would become a major-leaguer. He thought of his summer ballplaying as simply a brief hiatus from his true vocation of automobile mechanic, like his father, or possibly waiter, which he had been in a Clarksville, Ark., café in the 5:15 A.M. to 9 P.M. shift. He had earned enough money on tips at that café to pay his way to a tryout camp in the mid-Thirties, where he signed his third Class D contract, from which he was shortly thereafter released.

When Sain finally managed to put together two respectable seasons in pro baseball (he was 16 and 4 and 18 and 10 in successive years with Newport, another Class D team), his manager told him to bring a first-basemen's glove to spring training the following year. He had batted .315 as a part-time first-baseman and his manager was sure that was the only way Sain would ever make the majors. Luckily for Sain, many young pitchers were drafted to fight World War II that year (1941), so he was forced to remain a pitcher. That spring, after five years in Class D leagues and after having been released four times, Johnny Sain made the jump to the Double A Southern Association. The following spring he so impressed Boston Braves' manager Casey Stengel that Casey brought him north to start the 1942 season. At the time Johnny Sain was a quiet 25-year-old rookie with a good curveball, little speed and decent control. Used solely as a relief pitcher, Sain posted a 4 and 7 record and a 3.90 ERA before he, too, was drafted at the close of the 1942 season. He joined the Navy Air Corps that winter, along with Ted Williams, Joe Coleman and Johnny Pesky. However, true to form, Sain spent 22 months trying to earn his flight wings while the others earned theirs in less than a year. "I've always been a slow learner," says Sain today. "That's helped me a lot both as a player and coach. I have to go over things again and again before they stick in my mind. But when they do, they stick better than if I had picked them up real quick."

From 1942 to 1946 Sain pitched in various service leagues throughout the South, and those four years became, in effect, an extension of his minor league training. He used them wisely to develop an assortment of new breaking balls (sliders and various speed curveballs), to experiment with ways of setting up hitters and to prepare himself mentally for the moment when he returned to the major leagues. He improved so rapidly that at one point he struck out Ted Williams three consecutive times in a

188

service game. Still, when Sain returned to Boston in 1946, fans and writers alike expected little from the 29-year-old relief pitcher who had spent the equivalent of 10 years in the minors. Only his manager, Billy Southworth, noticed Sain's vast improvement, and he told sportswriters during spring training, "You'd better pay attention to Sain over there. He just might win 20 games this season."

Sain won 21 games in 1946 and lost 14. He posted a 2.21 ERA, the best of his career. Another Boston Braves' pitcher, 24-year-old Warren Spahn, managed only eight victories that same year, although he would soon overshadow Sain in notoriety (and longevity) if not in performance. Sain and Spahn pitched together for five years, from 1946 to 1950. Their fans believed the Braves could defeat any team in the world in a four-game series, provided only that the heavens blessed them with "Spahn and Sain and a day of rain." (Ironically, Sain was mentioned last because his name more aptly rimed with "rain," as if even the gods of posy had conspired against him). From 1946 to 1950 Johnny Sain won 94 games, Warren Spahn 85. However, it was the left-handed Spahn—younger, more ebullient, with that stylish form and classic repertoire (blazing fastball)—who captured the imagination of writers and fans. Even his profile deserved attention by its very sharpness, while Sain, older, more mature, soft-spoken, with only modest ability, seemed the epitome of blurred edges. Where Spahn was blazing, witty, outspoken, Sain was workmanlike, reliable, serious, and a man of few words. In fact, Sain was so reticent in those days that he failed to tell his wife, the former Doris McBride, he was a major league pitcher until months after their marriage. He also refused to contribute to team discussions whenever the topic concerned his methods for dispatching opposing batters. He had never been coached in the minor leagues (no one considered him enough of a prospect to waste the time) and had had to educate himself slowly, painstakingly over 10 years. And so he had grown quite protective of his hard-earned pitching knowledge.

Because of Sain's reputation for dependability (he seldom missed a turn on the mound even when his arm was sore) and his inherent unobtrusiveness, the baseball world of 1948 was somewhat stunned when that July, a few days before the All-Star game, Johnny Sain threatened to quit baseball. "I meant it," he says today. "I was gonna walk away from the whole thing." Sain had won 21 games in 1947 and 11 games by the 1948 All-Star game, and now he demanded that Braves' owner Lou Perini renegotiate his contract for $30,000. What had apparently angered the previously unflappable Sain was news that Perini had just shelled out almost $80,000 to a 17-year-old left-hander named Johnny Antonelli, while he, a proven 20-game winner, had had to settle for $21,500 that spring—a figure he had not been happy with even then. Eventually Sain got his $30,000 and a two-year contract to boot, but he had set a precedent for himself that he was to repeat numerous times over the next 10 years when negotiating both as a player and a coach.

It was not the money that mattered to the modest-living pitcher, but what it signified to him. Sain had gone unrecognized for so long, for one reason or another, that he had come to view the respect and loyalty his teams had for him in terms of their salary offers. How much could a team respect him and his talent, he wondered, if they gave an untried youth almost three times what they seemed willing to pay him? "When people take advantage of me," said Sain, "they set the rules and then I follow them, too." During the previous fall, for instance, Sain felt he had been taken advantage of by Cleveland's ace pitcher Bob Feller. He had promised Sain $2800 if he would pitch on a barnstorming team of professionals that Feller had organized. Sain agreed, but during that tour he seldom pitched. Most of the pitching was done by the more popular Feller, with his blazing fastball, and the flamboyant Satchel Paige, with his blazing personality, both of whom aroused much greater fan interest than would an appearance by that good gray workman, Johnny Sain. At the end of the tour Feller offered Sain $1800 and Sain accepted it, wordlessly. But that humiliation was still on his mind when he took the mound against Feller in the 1948 World Series, and it was with great satisfaction that he defeated Feller 1–0, to deprive him of the one laurel that escaped him throughout his career—a World Series victory.

Johnny Sain finished out his productive years as a relief pitcher with the New York Yankees from 1951 to 1955. He had been acquired by Casey Stengel, always a Sain admirer, who had willingly surrendered to the Braves a fidgety, freckle-faced right-hander named Lewis Selva Burdette. Sain's years with the Yankees were noteworthy for reasons other than his modest successes on the mound. He made a number of friends with the Yankee heroes of that era—Mantle and Ford and Berra—but most notable of these was his friendship with a light-hitting Army Ranger whose duty it was to warm him up in the bullpen before he went into a game to relieve. Ralph Houk, who came to bat 161 times in an eight-year career, spent most of his time in bullpens. But unlike many bullpen occupants, he put his time to good use. He studied each game carefully, discussed various situations with some of his pitchers, especially Sain, and diligently prepared himself for that day when he hoped he would be called upon to manage those same Yankees. Houk's diligence was eventually rewarded, and he was able to go from a nonplaying major-leaguer to a successful manager with little discomfort. And when he first made that transition he remembered Johnny Sain, whom he considered not only a friend but also a player whose pitching knowledge he respected greatly.

When Johnny Sain retired from baseball as an active player in 1955, he was admittedly a frustrated man. "It happens to all older major-leaguers," he says. "There are so many uncertainties confronting you—which game will be my last, what will I do now, why are people treating me differently? It's a very difficult period. I've always felt each club should have a reorientation program for their older players to teach them how to readjust to life outside of baseball."

The Johnny Sain who was caught up in his own frustrations and fading career in 1955, however, was vastly different from the Sain who became the Kansas City Athletics' pitching coach in 1959. "To become a pitching coach," says Sain, "you have to start all over again. You

have to get outside of yourself. You might have done things a certain way when you pitched but that doesn't mean it will be natural to someone else. For example, I threw a lot of sliders and off-speed pitches because I wasn't very fast. But that's me. I could also pitch with only two days' rest (he once pitched nine complete games in 29 days) whereas most pitchers need three and four, although I think they shouldn't. And I never believed much in running pitchers to keep them in shape. I've always felt a lot of pitching coaches made a living out of running pitchers so they wouldn't have to spend that same time teaching them how to pitch, something they were unsure of. It would be better to have those pitchers throw on the sidelines every day, than run. Things like this I learned on my own. I picked up everything by observation, which is the best teacher. Nothing came easy to me. I had to think things over and over more than guys with natural ability did. Maybe this has made it easier for me to get my ideas across to pitchers. It isn't that I'm so smart, because I know I'm not very smart at all. I don't know any answers. I don't give pitchers answers. I try to stimulate their thinking, to present alternatives and let them choose. I remind them every day of things they already know but tend to forget. I repeat things a lot, partly for them but also for my own thinking, to make sure what I'm saying makes sense. . . .
I don't make anyone be like Johnny Sain. I want them to do what's natural for them. I adjust to their style, both as pitchers and people. I find some common ground outside of baseball that'll make it easier for us to communicate in general. I used to talk flying with Denny McLain all the

time. Once you can communicate with a pitcher it's easier to make him listen to you about pitching. You know him better, too. You know when to lay off him, when to minimize his tensions, and also when to inspire him. That's why you've got to know him. Pitching coaches don't change pitchers, we just stimulate their thinking. We teach their subconscious mind so that when they get on the mound and a situation arises it triggers an automatic physical reaction that they might not even be aware of."

Sain lasted one full year with the Athletics, for which he was paid $12,000. Kansas City was then considered both a farm team and an elephant's burial ground for the powerful New York Yankees. It seemed, at the time, that every aging body the Yankees dispatched finished out his days with Kansas City (including Sain four years before), and that every talented youngster the A's produced somehow landed in New York to aid the Yankees in another pennant drive. (At Kansas City Sain worked with a young Ralph Terry and Bud Dailey, both of whom were eventually traded to the Yankees.) Sain resigned his position with the A's at the close of the 1959 season because, as he told sportswriters, he felt the organization wasn't trying to build for the future. "I didn't want to be someplace where I was putting more into an organization than that organization was." This dawned on him quite suddenly one day when he went to the office of the general manager, Park Carroll, and asked for four guest tickets to that day's game. Carroll produced the tickets and then asked Sain to pay for them. Sain paid and left the room thinking, "That sonofabitch! And after all I've given him for $12,000. Well, if they don't care that much about me, I'm going." Years later Sain would say with a grin, "If Park Carroll hadn't charged me for those tickets I might still be at Kansas City."

Sain sat out the 1960 baseball season in Bellview, Ark., where he now owned a new-car dealership. However, when he heard that his friend Ralph Houk had been appointed the Yankee manager for 1961, he knew he'd have a job in baseball again. Ralph Houk did not rehire long-time Yankee pitching coach Jim Turner. Instead, he hired his friend and former bullpen mate, Johnny Sain, for the 1961 season.

"Ralph and I got along as well as anybody could," says Sain today. "We thought alike about most things and we respected one another. We'd even gotten to the point of discussing family problems with each other."

At first things did not go well for new manager Ralph Houk. He was confronted with certain undefinable problems, as would any manager who had been a bullpen catcher on a team of Fords and Mantles and Berras and was then placed in a position of authority over those same men. In desperation Houk turned to Sain for help. Sain, the reliable, the tireless, the undaunted, the jouster with windmills, responded. One day after a particularly heartbreaking loss, Sain told a dispirited Houk, "Ralph, things look pretty dark for us right now, but don't let any sonofabitch know it. Let's not panic now." A few weeks later, when the Yankees moved into first place, Ralph Houk, puffing a cigar, told reporters, "Yeh, things looked pretty bad for me last month, but I wasn't about to let any sonofabitch know it."

Eventually the Yankees won pennants in 1961, 1962 and 1963, and a World Series championship in 1961 and 1962, under the managership of Ralph Houk who was named Manager of the Year in 1961. During that same period Whitey Ford, Ralph Terry and Jim Bouton became 20-game winners for the only times in their careers under the tutelage of Johnny Sain. Says Ford of Sain, "If you don't know a coach personally, you'd try his stuff once or twice and if it didn't work, you'd stop. But you get so personal with Sain, you admire the man so much, that you just have to give his ideas an extra chance. It was Sain teaching me a hard slider and pitching me with two and three days' rest instead of the four and five days I thought I needed before that made me a 20-game winner."

But despite their mutual successes, which should have enhanced their friendship, Johnny Sain and Ralph Houk began to drift apart. Houk confided in Sain less and less each year, and when he did it was seldom on a personal basis as it had been before. Sain, as usual, said little. It was during those years that Houk, the ex-Ranger, began to build a reputation as a forceful disciplinarian. (He flattened a slightly drunk Ryne Duren with one punch on the train that brought the victorious Yankees back to New York after their 1958 World Series victory.) Soon Houk was being referred to by fans and in newspapers as "The Major."

Jim Bouton, wearing bellbottoms and a body shirt of robin's egg blue, leans forward over his desk at WABC-

TV and says, "But does he still like me? I mean, after the book and all. Does Johnny still like me?" Assured, he sits back and says, "Johnny Sain taught me everything I know, from how to put on sanitary socks [inside out so as not to get a blister from the lint that forms in the toes] to how to negotiate a contract. I admire Sain more than any man I ever met. All players like Sain. Black, white, liberal, conservative, loud, quiet—they all do. Sain gets a pitcher's allegiance before any manager could. Managers don't like this. But it isn't Sain's fault. He doesn't try to undermine a manager's position. He can't help it if what he is appeals more to pitchers than what their managers are, can he? Johnny sees very deeply into things. A lot of managers can't stand to have him around after awhile. What general likes a lieutenant who's smarter than him? John has the ability to see right through a bull-shitter, which most managers are, to the essence of the man.

"Who wants to live with a guy like Sain, always standing off in the corner watching you, and every time you do some crappy thing to a player, there's John, not saying anything, not revealing what he sees, just looking like some knight in shining armor who knows all. Even if he never reveals what he sees, it becomes obvious to everyone. And then the manager loses face and blames Sain for it, although it isn't Sain's fault for seeing deeply, it's the managers fault for doing the things he does. If a manager can't admit to himself what he is, how do you think he feels knowing Johnny Sain sees it? Take Chuck Tanner, for instance. He's a nice guy who didn't know where the bodies were buried when he came to the White Sox. Now he's a successful manager—mostly because of Sain's help. How long do you think he'll want to look over his shoulder and see Sain reminding him, just by his presence, that he owes a good part of his success to him? It takes a big man to be able to live with that. That's why Ralph Houk got rid of Sain in '63. At first Houk sought out Sain for help because he was insecure. But when he became a successful manager, "The Major," he didn't need a talented coach anymore, especially one who reminded him that he owed part of his success to him. All he wanted was someone who was loyal, and Sain is loyal to himself first, his pitchers second and his manager third. Finally, when Houk quit and Berra took over, Houk was afraid Berra would be a winner with Sain's help and that would diminish Houk's success, so he got rid of Sain.

"The funny thing is that Johnny, who's supposed to be such a radical, is a real Establishment type. He gives you the perfect out to get rid of him. He's too goddamned nice and people take advantage of him. And jeez, he's so honest! So damned honest! If I was ever on trial for my life I'd want Johnny Sain on that jury, and then I'd be sure the truth would come out."

When the Yankees lost the 1963 World Series to the Dodgers in four straight games, John Sain found it strange that Ralph Houk, always a bitter loser, did not seem particularly upset by that humiliation. He knew why when he read in the newspapers that Ralph Houk had been promoted to general manager and Yogi Berra had replaced him as field manager for the 1964 season.

"Throughout 1963 I had seen Berra and Crosetti always huddling and whispering," says Sain today. "I knew something was up, but I waited for Ralph to tell me. I wanted Ralph to tell me. Then someone told me there was a rumor that Yogi would be the manager next year and I said, 'No way. The players won't respect him.' When I read about it in the papers I began thinking. Well, now Ralph Houk is a man I always thought leveled with me, and here he didn't tell me about Yogi until after I read it in the papers? Houk sent me a letter saying he hoped it wasn't too big a shock to me, and after that I got a letter from Yogi asking me to work for him next. I wrote Houk a letter saying that due to increased expenses I needed a $5000 raise from the $25,000 I was already getting, which at the time was the highest salary ever paid a pitching coach, I believe. I also told Ralph I needed a two-year contract, and that Yogi's biggest problem was going to be getting the respect of the players. Houk called me on the phone a few days later and said Topping wouldn't go for the extra money. I said, 'Okay, send me my release.' He did. If he had been my friend, like I thought, he would have tried to talk me out of leaving. But he didn't. He just sent my release a few days later. When Bouton found out about it in the papers, he offered to give me the extra money I was asking for out of his own salary. He thought it was just a salary dispute like the papers had indicated. I think, if I really wanted to, I could have stayed with the Yankees, but I walked away from it. Then they put Whitey in as pitching coach, and after him they put Jim Turner back in, and I know what Ralph Houk thinks of Jim Turner."

Ralph Houk, chewing a cigar, narrows his eyes and says in an emphatically flat voice, "Jim Turner is the best pitching coach ever. Understand? The best ever! A good pitching coach deals only with mechanics. It can be detrimental to a team if a pitching coach gets too personally involved with his pitchers. He should treat them mechanically. That's why Johnny Sain had his troubles. I've heard a lot of bad things about Sain since he left us. He can't seem to hold a job, can he? Jim Turner's been a pitching coach with the Yankees for years. He knows what I expect of him. We get together every day and I tell him how I'm gonna use the pitchers and he does it."

After Sain left the Yankees he was forced to sit out a year until, in the winter of 1965, Calvin Griffith, the owner of the Minnesota Twins, offered him a job.

"What about salary?" said Sain. "They say I'm a high-priced man."

"Anything you say will be all right with me, John," said Griffith.

Sain, who had been getting $25,000 a year from the Yankees, and who had demanded $30,000 a year, then signed with the Twins for $20,000 a year.

Before the 1965 season began it had been rumored that Twins' manager Sam Mele would lose his job if he did not produce a winner in 1965. When he first arrived at spring training, Sain remarked off-handedly, "Wouldn't it be funny if Mele became the Manager of the Year?" That year the Twins did win the American League pennant and Sam Mele was voted Manager of the Year.

Despite both Mele and Sain's success (Sain had produced his usual 20-game winner in Mudcat Grant, who said of him, "He sure puts biscuits in your pan"), the two men did not get along. Mele distrusted Sain and the power he wheeled over his pitchers. Furthermore, he seldom agreed with Sain's unorthodox pitching concepts, and often the two men would have words over the amount of running a pitcher should do, or how many days' rest he might need between starts. But beyond those differences, Sain felt he was never able to communicate deeply with Mele, that he never knew where he stood with him, which was fatal to a man like Sain, who seems physically unable to deal with people on only a superficial level. After signing a 1966 contract for $25,000, Sain's difficulties with Mele grew, until by mid-season they were irreconcilable. The final blow to their relationship came in mid-season when Billy Martin, then a Twins' coach, berated one of Sain's pitchers over a pitch he had just thrown. Sain, furious, said to Martin, "Mind your own business, Martin. I take care of the pitchers." Mele, who was standing beside Sain, said nothing. Later, thinking about the incident, Sain became more and more upset that Mele had not come to his defense against Martin's intrusion into his private domain. The following afternoon Johnny Sain moved all his equipment and uniforms out of the coaches' locker room and deposited the lot in the players' locker room, where he dressed until the end of the season, when he was fired.

When news of Sain's dismissal was made public, Jim Kaat, a 25-game winner under Sain that year, wrote an open letter to the Twins' front office, which was published in a Minnesota newspaper. The letter accused the Twins of making a terrible mistake in firing Sain, and it implied that the team's drop to second place that year was because of Mele's inability to communicate with his players, as well as with Sain.

Dave Boswell, now an infrequent relief pitcher for the Baltimore Orioles and a pitcher at Minnesota in 1966, is sitting on a stool in front of his locker. He was once a 20-game winner with the Twins but has since damaged his arm so severely that he was given his unconditional release by the Twins and was picked up by the Orioles only on a gamble. "If Johnny Sain had any weakness as a pitching coach," says Boswell, "it was that he didn't understand hard throwers as much as he should. He never made us run wind sprints at Minnesota because he didn't believe in running. Some of the pitchers, me and Kaat in particular, didn't run 10 sprints all year, and we came up with sore arms. But that was our fault, I guess. Johnny left it up to us to run on our own if we thought we needed it. That was what was so great about him. He never pressured you to do anything. He didn't bother you a lot, but when he did, when he talked about pitching and the possibilities of a baseball, you could actually see them before your eyes. As a kid you put that ball in your hand and you thought of it as just a ball. But after Sain put that ball in your hand you didn't see it the same anymore. Now it had possibilities you never dreamed of."

From 1967 to 1969 Johnny Sain coached under Mayo Smith at Detroit. In 1968 the Tigers won the American League pennant and the World Series; Mayo Smith was named Manager of the Year; Denny McLain became the first pitcher to win 30 or more games in one season since Dizzy Dean turned that trick in 1934; and Mickey Lolich won three complete games in the World Series to become only the seventh man in baseball history to accomplish that feat. Ironically, but predictably enough, Sain became close friends with Lolich and McLain, both of whom he had been warned were "real nuts," while he grew daily more estranged from Mayo Smith, who he had been told "was a real gentleman."

"McLain and Lolich both wanted to improve themselves," says Sain, "and that's all I need in a man. Each was very individualistic, too, and I like that. McLain may have been a little loose off the mound, but on that mound he was all business. And he's got guts. Him and Lolich, both. You know that Lolich rides those motorcycles of his, and McLain, he's got a pilot's license. If McLain was flying an airplane and it died on him, you could bet money he'd still be fighting it when it hit the ground. But it was Mayo I had problems with. He's a helluva fine guy like everybody told me, and I only really disagreed with him once. But still we never got along. When I came to Detroit I had a reputation behind me, and he was relatively unknown and trying to make a name for himself. Every day

203

the writers and TV sportscasters would seek me out for an interview. They were always asking me questions—like why didn't I become a manager, which I could never be— and all the time Mayo was hitting that pressroom trying to be a real nice guy with reporters. Pretty soon I could sense there was friction there, between Mayo and me. I don't like friction. It lingers with me, even small things. It disturbs me if I have to be on my toes with someone, always afraid I might offend him. That's not what life's all about. And Mayo had this ability to keep me uneasy all the time. He was so smooth I never knew where I stood with him. I'd rather he declared himself, cuss me out, so we could get things into the open. But he never did. He was always a real nice guy with me."

Mickey Lolich, a 25-game winner with the Tigers in 1971, sits down for breakfast at the Hotel Roosevelt in New York City and orders four scrambled eggs, four pieces of toast, an order of bacon, a large orange juice and a pot of coffee. At six feet, 230 pounds, Lolich refers to himself as a fat man's athlete. "Fat guys need idols, too," he once said. Now, speaking softly and occasionally glancing across to a nearby table where his manager, Billy Martin, is eating his breakfast, Lolich talks about Johnny Sain. "He made me a 20-game winner. Yet he never taught me a single thing about pitching a baseball. Maybe that's because John's not a pitching coach, he's a head-shrinker. He used to straighten out all those hardship cases, you know, mental cases, in flight school when he was a Navy flier in the Forties. Even when you learn from Sain you never feel you've learned a thing from him. He lets you think you did it yourself. McLain wouldn't learn from anyone when he was with Detroit, so Johnny just taught him things without letting Denny know it. McLain used to sneak down to the bullpen like a little kid so he cold practice what Sain had taught him without letting anyone know it. I'll bet to this day he'll swear he never learned a thing from Johnny. But every pitcher learns from John. Pitching takes on new shades and nuances with Sain. He loves pitchers. Maybe he doesn't love baseball so much, but he loves pitchers. That's why he doesn't get along with management. He believes pitchers are unique and only he understands them. If the front office tries to trade a guy, he goes to that guy's defense. He always sides with pitchers first. In the end it gets him in trouble. I think he has this dream that someday a manager will say to him, 'Here, Johnny, you take the pitchers. They're all yours.' "

In the spring of 1970, after he had been fired from the Detroit Tigers, Sain was offered the job of minor league pitching coach with the California Angels. He was offered that job by Roland Hemmond, the club's farm director and a son-in-law of John Quinn, a former executive with the old Boston Braves during Sain's days with that club. (A year later Hemmond would become the director of player personnel with the Chicago White Sox, and he would bring with him Chuck Tanner and Johnny Sain.) To the surprise of most of the baseball world, Sain accepted Hemmond's offer. He spent much of the 1970 season driving across the country, stopping at cities like El Paso, Clinton,

Salt Lake City and Idaho Falls, where he worked with youngsters who were light-years away from the Lolichs and McLains he had been accustomed to. Yet Sain cherishes that experience in which, in his own words, "I rediscovered the country. I had been having marriage problems and I took that job to get away from things. I'd always thought that in baseball or in life you get to a point where you can relax, level off, but I found out you can never rest. You always have the possibility of sinking. This divorce action with my wife has made me stay young as I grow older. She's got four lawyers and she's determined to take my money, my kids and my reputation, and I'm just as determined not to let her. I guess I had always let her do whatever she wanted before. At 50 she wanted to go back to college so I encouraged her. But then she seemed to think she was better than me. We always seemed to be in competition. She said I was too easy and I liked to be kicked around by people. Maybe she's right. But still, this whole divorce action is very destructive. It's not only destructive to me and our four kids, but it's destructive to her as a person. Why, I took care of my wife's grandparents for years, and when they died I buried them. And I buried her father, too.

"It seems the more responsibility a man takes the more he gets. I've been taking care of people all my life. We're all looking for someone who will stick with us. But all I've ever got from people was, 'You could never do this,' or 'You could never do that.' I was always an outsider. I was never anyone's glamour boy. I was always looking over my shoulder at some new Dizzy Dean who would make everyone forget me. People were always waiting to drive a nail in my coffin. It's a human weakness to hope somebody fails. But people are never the way you're taught they should be. We grow up with standards that we find aren't true. I always thought if you were straight with people they would be straight with you. But they aren't. Still, you have to be straight with them. I hate for people to toy with me, to be superior, but I've got to give them the chance. I don't know why I'm always testing people, but I am. Maybe I'm just playing games with them. Maybe I'm fooling everyone."

Johnny Sain, wearing the bluish-gray traveling uniform of the Chicago White Sox, stands with arms folded behind Steve Kealey, who is working steadily off the pitcher's mound behind home plate at Fenway Park in Boston. Kealey sweats and grunts as he throws. He is 23 years old. He has red hair, freckles and the muscled, tapering build of a swimmer. While he sweats Sain talks softly to him. Kealey makes no acknowledgment of Sain's words, which are few, really only a phrase, an exhortation, rarely a sentence.

"Heh, that had the beginnings," says Sain. "The beginnings." Kealey, impassive, continues to throw a curveball that is flat and does not break down as much as Sain would wish. "He'll get it soon enough," says Sain, loud enough for Kealey to hear. "It's just a matter of time." Kealey throws another curveball that breaks down slightly.

"Heh, that's real nice," says Sain. He motions to Tommy John walking by. "Wasn't that real nice, Tommy?"

It is mid-July and Kealey is 1 and 1 with an ERA of 4.39. He is a hard thrower with decent control, but even he will be the first to admit he is far from being a finished pitcher. But he has confidence that wherever his potential might lie, Sain will unearth it. "He tells me things I never considered before," says Kealey through dazed eyes. "They make sense when you think about them, but who ever thinks of the things Johnny Sain does. John's whole life is teaching pitchers. It's like by teaching us to get hitters out it proves he could have done it today, too. You know, his success lives on."

After Kealey finishes throwing, Sain will walk to the outfield where the rest of the Chicago pitchers are standing around, stirring themselves infrequently to retrieve a fly ball in a half-hearted lope, but more often planted, spread-legged, like gray-flanneled pelicans. Sain will move from pitcher to pitcher, from left field to center to right and then back again. He will stand beside each one for a few moments, his arms folded across his chest, spitting tobacco juice into the still, sunny afternoon, passing the time in small talk that only occasionally drifts into then out of the subject of pitching.

Sain will say very little about pitching to Wilbur Wood, the club's 30-year-old knuckleballer, because as Sain admits, "I don't know much about knuckleballs." Wood, a chunky, smiling, tobacco-chewing man, is an eight-year veteran who had been cast off by the Red Sox and the Pirates, both of whom used him primarily as a relief pitcher. Last year as a reliever with the White Sox he was 9 and 13. The club's 1971 brochure said that "some thought was being given to restoring him to a starting role on occasion." That thought belonged to Sain. He made one other suggestion to Wood, and it was that he pitch often with only two days' rest between starts. Sain felt that as a knuckleballer, Wood put less strain on his arm than did other pitchers with more orthodox stuff, and therefore he could absorb the extra work with ease. Wood started 42 games in 1971 and won 22 of them. He pitched 334 innings, the most of any White Sox pitcher since 1917 and second in the American League in 1971 to Mickey Lolich's 376 innings. Wood's ERA was 1.91, second in the league to Vida Blue's 1.82.

Sain will also say very little to Vincente Romo, the club's 28-year-old Mexican-born relief pitcher, but for a different reason. Romo, a syrupy-smooth–skinned man who resembles an overweight bullfighter, is another Red Sox castoff. He possesses an elaborate windmill motion (similar to Luis Tiant's) that seems to deliver a thousand different pitches from a thousand different angles. He also speaks little English, and for this reason Sain finds it difficult to communicate with him as deeply as he'd like. With Romo he deals primarily with pitching mechanics. To speak to him in more personal terms would be to risk a misunderstanding, says Sain. The limits imposed on him in his relationship with Romo disturb Sain, and from time to time he will admit, "I wish I could get closer to him." Last year, his first with the Sox, Romo was 1 and 7.

Sain talks a good deal with Joel Horlen, the club's 34-year-old, 10-year veteran. Horlen, a small, soft-spoken man with a preoccupied gaze, is at a crucial juncture in his career. He was once the ace of the Chicago staff, winning 19 games in 1967, but has fallen on hard times of late as he has lost speed from both his fastball and his curveball. Sain is trying to help Horlen make that adjustment all pitchers must make in their mid-30s, when the quality of their pitches deteriorates and so they must add to their pitching repertoire. Sain is working with Horlen on a screwball, which he hopes will prolong his career. "He doesn't say much to guys who are going good," says Horlen. "He's a funny guy. He seems to spend more time with guys who are having their problems. Like he always says, he waits for guys to hit bottom before he talks to them." After a 6 and 16 season in 1970, Horlen posted an 8 and 9 record in 1971, his first year under Sain.

Rich Hinton, a 22-year-old graduate of the University of Arizona, has pitched only one inning in this his first major league season. Yet Johnny Sain calls him a terrific prospect, if for no other reason than "he looks at you real straight." Of Sain, Hinton says, "Working under John is the best break I could get. Every club he's been with has had a 20-game winner. The only problem is that he's been with so many clubs that all the pitchers he's taught cut each others' throats. It's like telling everyone in a card game the same trick. Pretty soon they'll all use it and nobody benefits. What I like best about John, though, is that he never second-guesses you. He'll come out to the mound and say, 'Don't you worry, that was a helluva pitch. He never should have hit it.' Then he'll say, 'Now this batter is a poor breaking ball hitter, but you can throw him whatever you think best. You're the judge.' And when you get the guy out with a breaking ball you believe it was your pitch, not his. You made that final decision. Johnny Sain lets you make the act of will."